The Bowen Island Arts Council
Box 211
Bowen Island
British Columbia
V0N 1G0

Howe Sounds
ISBN 0-9699090-0-4

Typeset and Printed in Canada

HOWE
SOUNDS

Fact, fiction and fantasy
from the writers of Bowen Island

Edited by
Richard Littlemore

Acknowledgments

In addition to the authors, all of whom volunteered their time and donated their work for this book, there are several others deserving of the warmest thanks. Nick Bantock, whose latest work is reproduced beginning on page 105, made a double contribution by also designing this book's cover. Ralph Lubin assisted in production and Jim Emerson and David McLean were extremely helpful in typographic design and layout. Joanne Blain's proofreading skills were invaluable, and if any typos remain, I must have inserted them after her last check.

None of this work would have seen print, however, if not for the perseverence of Alixe Matthew in rounding up financing and the generosity of these Bowen Island patrons: A.C. Angus, Sue Barr, Lois McLaren, Thomas Nesbitt, the W.K. (Bill) Russell family, Peter Schmidt and Derek Stuart.

Finally, I would like to thank my wife, Elizabeth, for her proofreading and her editing advice, but even more for her support and encouragement, without which this book would not have been possible.

Richard Littlemore
Editor

It's impossible to say why so many writers are attracted to Bowen Island, whether they come for inspiration or refuge, or whether any two writers come for the same reason. But since the days when Earle Birney and Jane Rule gathered here in a writers' commune dubbed Lieben, Bowen has provided at least a part-time home for a remarkable array of literary talent.

This book is intended to celebrate that talent — to applaud the accidental collection of writers and poets, of essayists and academics, of humourists and wry observers of life. It also is intended as a literary sampler, a smorgasbord of writers and styles that will appeal to every taste and pander to every preference.

For those unfamiliar with our home, Bowen Island is the grand mass that stops up the mouth of Howe Sound, just north of Vancouver. It coddles a year-round population of between 2,500 and 3,000 people — depending on whether you're listening to a real estate salesman or a Gulf Island recluse — and it entertains a further population of summer and weekend residents. It boasts two pubs, three churches, a good bookstore, a fine library and the rancorous politics of any small town.

Bowen's prodigious cultural community flourishes in the hands of the Bowen Island Arts Council, whose president, Albert McLane, inspired this anthology. All the work that appears here was donated by the authors and all proceeds of the book will go to the Arts Council.

So, read and enjoy. We hope that you find a few of your favourite writers within these pages and that you discover some new ones, as well. On Bowen Island, or in the local library, there is much more where this came from.

Contents

Fact, Philosophy and Food

ROBERT BRINGHURST
Fast Drumming Ground 3
CHARLOTTE TOWNSEND-GAULT
Northwest Coast Art: The Culture of the Land Claims.......13
VICTOR CHAN
Tibetan Concepts of Pilgrimage..29
NEIL BOYD
Just Say No to a War Against Drugs...................................39
IAIN BENSON
Goodness, Values and Community: Compasses
with Damaged Needles..............51
PETER CLARKE
Thatcherism: The Downing Street Years............................67
BRAD OVENELL-CARTER
Play Dough..75

Fiction

MARIA TIPPETT
Going the Wrong Way..81
TERESA PLOWRIGHT
Making History..89

Fantasy

NICK BANTOCK
The History of Imaginary Spinning Tops..........................105

Poetry

JULIE OVENELL-CARTER
Food Fight...119

Just Too Personal to Categorize

LISA HOBBS BIRNIE
Reflections on the Light...123
VALERIE LUPINI
The B.A.F.U. Club...127
PASCAL GUILLON
Montenegro by Mistake..135
JIM KEARNEY
The Good Old Days..145
RICHARD LITTLEMORE
How Now Brown Cow?..149

ROBERT BRINGHURST

The list of accomplishments in Robert Bringhurst's curriculum vitae would have exhausted three or four lesser mortals. He is a much-published and widely acclaimed writer of poetry and prose, and an experienced hand in writing for the stage and for radio. He has lectured in universities in Canada, Australia, New Zealand, Japan, Fiji, Austria, Spain, Germany, Portugal, Italy, the United Kingdom and Ireland.

Bringhurst has been a consulting editor and typographer for various publishing houses and his book, *The Elements of Typographic Style*, sets a new standard for scholarly work in the field. He has served as general editor for Kanchenjunga Press, of San Francisco and Vancouver, and as contributing editor for *Fine Print* magazine in San Francisco. He has also received numerous grants, fellowships and awards for his work.

It is disappointing, and perhaps perverse in a book of Bowen Island writers, to note that Bringhurst recently has sold his house and moved into Vancouver. The cache, which he refers to in the story that follows, has, in his words, "been dematerialized." The circumstances are extenuating and, we trust, temporary. Read this piece and judge for yourself whether Robert Bringhurst will return to Bowen Island.

Fast Drumming Ground

Home is alive, like a tree, not skinned and dressed or cut and dried like the quarried stone and milled wood that houses are made of, nor masticated and spat out like the particleboard and plywood used for packaging prefabricated lives. A house is not a home the way a mask is not a face. But a mask is not a mask if it can't be read as a metaphor for the face, and a house is not a house if it can't be seen as the mask of a home. Home is the whole earth, everywhere and nowhere, but it always wears the masks of particular places, no matter how often it changes or moves.

Mine moves often, but like many hunter-gatherers, I also keep a cache and circle back to it every year. I keep it now on a little island in what used to be the Squamish country, north and west of the rich new city of Vancouver — the third most populous city in the second most spacious country in the world, though it is barely a century old. Things have changed that much that fast.

The old name, the Squamish name, for this overshadowed island is *Xwlíl'xhwm:* a stony protuberance of meaning cloaked in a forest of evergreen consonants which I think is worth learning to pronounce.

Bowen Island, its English name, was given it by a Captain Richards, who charted the coast of southern British Columbia for the British Navy in 1859. His predecessor, George Vancouver, had already named the surrounding waters Howe Sound, to honour a British lord of the Admiralty, Richard Howe — Black Dick, his seamen liked to call him. Howe earned geographical immortality, in the British Admiralty's view, on 1 June 1794, by defeating a French fleet in the English Channel

3

— for which, of course, the French have a different name. The battle itself was known to British patriots as "the Glorious First of June." To the French, it was the 13th day of the month of Prairial, Year II of the Republic, and merely one more in a series of disasters that beset the Girondin and Jacobin regimes. Names are not the only things that vary with your point of view.

Captain Richards picked up the theme, naming other features within Howe Sound after British officers and ships involved in the same battle. Rear-Admiral James Bowen was one whom Richards chose to memorialize. Gambier, Bowyer and other nearby islands take their names from British officers who fought the French on the same day. Even Keats Island is named for a British admiral, not for the poet who wrote that "Heard melodies are sweet, but those unheard / Are sweeter," and that "true imagination ... has no self; it is everything and nothing." The poet, but not the admiral, so far as we know, struggled all his life to learn to listen to the world, and to unlearn "the Wordsworthian or egotistical sublime."

I want the names with which I touch the land I live in to connect me to that land. What most of them do instead is record the means by which its former inhabitants were evicted and their long-lived cultures destroyed. The way names link us to the land is not through history, which is sectarian and time-bound, but through myth, which works the other way around. History becomes myth when imagination edits it, and a glorified version of British military history was myth enough for captains Vancouver and Richards. But the Glorious First of June is not the myth I want to relive as I cross Queen Charlotte Strait to Bowen Island and walk beneath the alder and redcedar and hemlock and wild cherry, over the salmon stream and up along the deer trail that passes next to my door. Nor is it a myth I would like to bequeath to my neighbours or my children to relive. I think my friend, the historian Calvin Martin, is right when he says George Santayana was wrong: it is not those who forget history, it is instead those who *remember* it, who are compelled to go through it again.

Black Dick, Rear-Admiral Bowen and the others were all, no doubt, fine sailors and honourable men. I'd admire them if I met them. I nevertheless find little nourishment in thinking about their illustrious careers. And I prefer to derive my excitement from some other source than a one-day battle in La Manche two centuries ago, no matter who beat whom. On a diet of British military history, no matter how subtle and brilliant the tactics, no matter how noble the soldiers and sailors, as the pride swells, the mind and spirit starve.

For perhaps 10,000 years, the fjord I live in was a living map of the universe to the Salish-speaking peoples who were born and died here. It was a self-renewing library of archetypal images and stories as well as a self-replenishing larder of food, building materials, clothing and tools. It fed, sheltered and exercised body and mind. Its place names recorded the doings of Xhais, the transformer, who adjusted the world in such a way that no creature had too much power over another. Xhais, who could cut himself up and put himself back together again, often took the form of four brothers, shamans who sometimes altered themselves in turn into three human beings and a two-headed sealskin canoe. At other moments, they merged into one four-legged creature, usually a black bear.

The land was thick with other stories — not of distant struggles for money and power, but of the roots of being and time: how the Son of the Day emerged from a lake to marry the selfish shaman's daughter; how a man named Xwuch'tal' was roused on his wedding night at Stawamus to hunt the double-headed serpent, and how he made potent jewelry and weapons from its bones; how the Mosquito persuaded the Thunder that blood comes from wood instead of from flesh, which is why the lightning now strikes trees instead of people — and why my wisest neighbours never curse the mosquitoes.

These islands now are a cemetery of names for admirals who never sailed into this country. Their only connection with it lies in the fact that their victory over the French helped to secure the money and power by which the British conducted their colonization of Canada, in the successful pursuit of further money and power. The slopes looking down on Howe Sound are mangy now with the scars of clear cut logging. The waters are fouled with dioxins — leaving the prawns, crabs and other crustaceans inedible — because of poisons discharged by the pulp mills fed by that logging. The shellfish contaminate other creatures in turn, from seabirds to whales. It is so because we continue to believe, as generations of eager colonists have believed, that the land is ours instead of us, that it is merely there for the taking.

How many names the island has had, over how many thousand years of human habitation and migration through this area, is something we don't know, though we might begin to learn. The traces left by people living wisely in a land like this are slight, and not much archaeology has been done. In the meantime, I know what the island was called by those who lived here when Captain Richards visited and christened it for Admiral James Bowen. The earlier name, Xwlíl'xhwm, is used even now by people who speak the Squamish language, and it will stand for all the other names the island has worn over the centuries, and for the nameless smells and shapes by which it is known to the herons and eagles and ravens and gulls to whom it is home. If spoken names are sweet, are unspoken ones still sweeter? One name is a slender thread, but this one leads to a real world. It leads to a world that is real in a way the present world isn't, even though that other world has vanished and this one seems to thrive.

I call that world real because, through all its changes, it remained essentially self-sustaining instead of self-destructive. Its last transformation began when the Europeans arrived with too many answers and too few questions, and began to plant their flags. But I have a hunch that if this world lives, it will have to be by including among its models the very worlds it deliberately destroyed.

• • •

Xwlíl'xhwm means Fast Drumming Ground. Charles Hill-Tout, an English physician who lived in Vancouver and worked throughout southwestern British Columbia as an amateur archaeologist and ethnologist, heard the name from his Squamish acquaintances in the 1890s. Louis Miranda, one of the last not only fluent but eloquent speakers, and perhaps the only writer, in the Squamish language, taught the same name to a linguist named Aert Hendrik Kuipers in the 1960s.[1] The root is *lixhw*, which means to beat rapidly. (The *x* is a sound like the *ch* is in the German word *ich*. The *w* is a swallowed round vowel, an *o* that is never let out of the bag. The second syllable *líl'*, has a long accented vowel, like the *ee* in peel, and a glottal stop at the end — like the little catch in the throat that begins each syllable in the English expression of worry, *uh-oh*. The *xh* is like the ch in the German *Bach* or the Scottish *loch* — farther back in the throat than the *x* at the beginning. Add another suppressed round vowel, then *m*, and you'll have it: *Xwlíl'xhwm*.)

Kwum'shnam is the Squamish name for Hood Point, at the north end of Xwlíl'xhwm; it means Thumping Feet. Passage Island, just south of Xwlíl'xhwm, was called Smetlmetlel'ch. The old name for Gambier Island seems to be lost, though we still have the names for some of its bays and the seasonal village, St'ap'as, that stood on its northwest shore. Anvil Island was Tlaxwm. When Captain Vancouver rechristened it, naming it for its shape, there were plenty of knowledgeable Squamish still around, but questions like *What is your name for that island?* and *What does the name mean?* evidently never entered his mind. If they did, they must have seemed too much trouble to ask.

Many of the old names for the mountains around the fjord have vanished too. Miranda remembered that Mount Garibaldi was called Ta Nch'qai', "The Grimy One," in summer, but he did not tell Kuipers, and no one has told me, its winter name.

Ch'axhai' was the name for what is now called Horseshoe Bay. It was a village once, with a small and beautiful harbour. As all Bowen Islanders know, it's a ferry terminal now, primarily chain-link fence and asphalt, where thousands of travellers seeking nourishment and news are confronted by banks of silent machines dispensing junk paper and junk food. Each time I pass through it, I think of the colour, the talk, the fresh, hot, homemade food, and the anthology of faces in a hundred marketplaces and quayside lanes in South America, Africa, Asia, even in Europe — wherever the pre-industrial world is still permitted to spill through the fences. Though the population was small, that iridescent complexity greeted the first white visitors to the Squamish country too. In the name of efficiency, safety, privacy — all the synonyms of control — where we might have enriched it, we have chased it out and closed it down.

Q'iq'lxhn was the name of a fishing site on the other side of the Sound. Now it's the largest single source of pollutants in the local air and water. It's the site of the pulp mill at Port Mellon.

"Do they eat gold?" the Inca asked, watching the Spaniards stripping the temples. And the Squamish, when they saw Vancouver and his sailors in 1792, said *'U 'iu'aiti stiwaqin 'ia'wit, nitlch' mukwtnswit tiwa, wetl mnhwismatl ti s'atsuswit 'i'usxwixwi'.* "Maybe these are the dead, and those are their burial clothes, since only their faces are visible."[2]

• • •

Passage Island, Smetlmetlel'ch, is, I think, where the Xhais brothers were welcomed into the Squamish country. Far upstream on the Squamish River, they were bid farewell. And every episode in the never-quite-finished epic of creation was mapped onto someplace in between. Xwlíl'xhwm, I think, is where they created the Deer, Gambier where they created the Great Blue Heron, and Anvil Island, Tlaxwm, where the eldest brother snared the Sun. But there is no right and wrong distribution of stories. We can be sure the old storytellers themselves did not all agree on the sequence of episodes, nor the site of each episode. Even in an oral culture, the books move around on the shelves.

When the brothers first came to the country, things were too homogeneous. Perhaps, in fact, things were rather like they are now. The animals were indistinguishable one from another, like shrinkwrapped meat or the contents of tins. But they weren't dismembered and packaged. They simply looked like animals do when they're skinned. They looked like humans. The brothers themselves were disguised as three humans and a sealskin canoe. When they came ashore on Xwlíl'xhwm, they met a man who was sharpening a bone.

"What are you up to?" they asked.

"Making arrow points," said the man. "I've heard that someone is coming to change us. When he arrives, I intend to kill him."

"It's true," said the brothers, seizing the man. "Someone is coming."

They pulled at his ears, his arms, his neck, his jowls, and stretched and squeezed his fingers and toes. They twisted his hips up and his shoulders down. Then they planted two pieces of driftwood on his head and clapped their hands to chase him off. He became the deer, but he ran so fast the brothers feared he could never be caught. They chased him and knocked his hoofs together to slow him down. And they thrust the bone he had been working on into his foot, where it remains, the deer's astragalus bone, which looks like a half-worked spearpoint. Then they chased him away again.

"That will do," they said. "He is slow enough now, but not too slow." Then they went on.

Crossing to Cha'lkwnach, one of the south-facing bays on Gambier island, they met an old man fishing with a two-pronged spear. That is to say, he appeared to be fishing, but he was not really spearing his fish. He was rubbing the head of his spear against the bodies of the fish, then wiping the slime off the spear with moss and putting the moss and fish slime into his basket, letting the fish themselves swim off.

One of the brothers produced a barbed point and fixed it to the old man's spear, then speared a fish and held it up in front of the old man's eyes.

"Grandfather, this is the proper way to fish," said the brothers.

"Don't tell me what to do," the old man answered. "I prefer the slime."

"That is not how it ought to be, Grandfather," they said.

The brothers broke his spear in two and stuck the two halves to his legs. They stretched his neck, glued feathers to his hands, and fastened the spearpoint to his face, in place of his nose. Then they clapped their hands, and the old man rose unsteadily into the air. The brothers called him the Great Blue Heron.

They kept on paddling, and when they landed under a steep bluff on Tlaxwm, the youngest resumed his human form. There the four built a house near the mouth of a stream.

"I want to talk to the Sun," said the eldest brother. "I'm going to snare him."

That morning, he tied a line around the legs of his youngest brother, who turned himself into a salmon and danced in the stream. Not long after that, the Sun came down in the form of an eagle. Sound asleep in the heat of the day, the three older brothers saw nothing and heard nothing. The eagle made off with the salmon, snapping the line.

When the three brothers awoke in the cool of the evening, the eldest refused to allow any grieving. During the night, he braided a heavier cedarbark line. Next morning he tied it to the ankles of his second youngest brother, who leaped into the sea as a harbour seal.

The Sun came down again at noon that day in the form of an eagle, sinking his talons into the seal's back. The two older brothers slept and the eagle flew off with the seal, stretching and snapping the line.

Once again the eldest brother sat up all night braiding a line. He finished the thick cord late that morning and tied it to the ankles of his one remaining brother, who threw himself into the sea in the form of a porpoise.

That day at noon, the eagle descended again, and as the eldest brother slept in the great heat, the eagle of the Sun flew off, clutching his prey, stretching and snapping the heavy line.

That night, the eldest brother braided yet another cord and tied it to his own feet. When morning came, he slid into the sea, taking the form of a killer whale.

Noon came, and the Sun came down in the form of an eagle, sinking his talons into the whale's back. The eagle flapped his wings, but nothing happened. The whale was too heavy to lift. Then the whale took the eagle under the waves.

"Could we have a little chat now?" asked the whale.

"We could," said the eagle.

They returned to the surface, where Xhais and the Sun both took their human forms. Then they entered the house of the four brothers.

"What I want to know," Xhais said, "is where the salmon come from."

"A long way over there," the Sun said, pointing west with his luminous hand. "Where the rainbow-coloured smoke rises over the houses."

"How do I go there?" Xhais asked.

"Take the leaves of all the trees," the Sun said. "Take the roots of all the plants, the feathers of all the birds, and the bones of all the animals. That is the medicine you will need."

The Sun resumed his eagle form and flew up through the clouds. And Xhais collected everything, just as the Sun had said. Then he set off.

He paddled west for days, to where the sea is covered with floating charcoal, then to the place where the sea is covered with foam. Days after that, he saw smoke in all the colours of the rainbow rising to the clouds. Beneath the smoke was a line of houses.

The headman of the town was called Chinook Salmon. When Xhais arrived, Chinook Salmon called four of his villagers, two men and two women.

"Swim to the trap," he said. And the four of them stepped into the creek, turning to salmon as soon as their faces entered the water. Swimming upstream, they were caught in the trap behind the headman's house. And the villagers gaffed them, cleaned them, cut them and roasted them over the fire.

Xhais saw how the villagers buried the guts of the fish when they were cleaned, and how they set the flesh to cook by the fire. He shared in the feast, and he saw how the villagers gathered the skin and bones after the meal, and how they scattered them like the ashes of the dead on the water of the stream. Next morning, the four villagers who had turned into salmon and been eaten reappeared. But Xhais had kept a rib from the fish he had eaten. And one of the four who reappeared that morning had an open wound in his chest. He was moaning in pain.

Xhais went to the stream and lay his salmon bone down on the water. When he turned back to the village, he saw that the wounded one had been healed.

"Let me invite you to visit my country," Xhais said. And he gave Chinook Salmon a leaf from every tree, a root from every plant, a feather from every bird, a bone from every animal that lives in the Squamish country. Every year since then, the salmon have come. Most years, all five families of the salmon people come: the Chinook, the Sockeye, the Coho, the Dog, and finally the Pink. But even in the old days, the Pinks and the Dogs were sometimes mistreated and failed to return.

"Also, I need directions," Xhais said, "to the house of the Sun, where my brothers were taken."

"Go with the mouse, the louse and the flea," the Salmon said. "They know the way to the house of the Sun, and they know what to do when you arrive.

Xhais set off with these three for companions, over the mountains of white cloud and the ocean of air. They arrived at the Sun's house in the evening.

"The Sun will see you and hear you and smell you," said the mouse. "You should wait out here."

The mouse and the louse and the flea went under the door as soon as the Sun lay down for the night, and they kept him awake until morning. At dawn, when they let him alone, he fell into a deep sleep, and the house shook with his snoring. Then they opened the door to Xhais. And Xhais entered the Sun's house and gathered his dead brothers' bones.

He returned to his country. When he arrived, he covered his brothers' bones with a quilt of feathers and leaves. And after the Sun had passed through the sky four times, and the elder brother had danced on the beach for four days, the quilt stirred and his younger brothers revived.

They continued up the Sound, changing one thing and another. Long ago, they could still be seen, rearranging the mountains and snowfields around the upper reaches of the rivers.

• • •

There was a chapter in the story, once, for every animal important in the Squamish world, and for every cove and bay and cliff on every island and both shores of the sound. The people who fished and travelled and lived in this fjord relived as they did so, day by day, an epic of creation and an ethic of interdependence instead of reviewing Lord Howe's and Admiral Bowen's claims to military glory. No one ever told the story all at once, and maybe no one knew it all, but as each storyteller's knowledge of the world he lived in deepened, his story deepened too.

Some of the story — crucial as the missing salmon bone — is lost now, though its niche in the ecology is real. In time — when the canned meat and the frozen pizzas run out — replacement stories will evolve, if there is still a living watershed here for stories to evolve in. I know a few new ones even now, about another transformer called White Man, who split not into four but into millions of little white men, all of them busily rearranging the world. In one version, they kept rearranging the world more and more thoroughly, faster and faster, until there was simply no world left, only metal and plastic and petrochemicals and sand. In another, they changed it around until nothing quite worked anymore, and when that had happened, they soon got bored and wandered off.

Then the world sat there, homogenized, stunned, until one day a black bear wandered down from the Coast Mountains and tried to start conversations with rusting automobiles and empty junk food machines. He found they had nothing to say and weren't good to eat either, so he decided to rearrange and rename things. He changed himself into three human brothers and one canoe, they say, and started up the sound.

For those of us whose tongues come from Western Europe — even if the rest of our bodies were born in North America — the old name for the island is more difficult to spell than Bowen Island, and more difficult to say. It won't make the real estate move more briskly or increase the tourist flow. It isn't enough, by itself, even to make us think very much about the people who used to live here and the way they used to live. But I prefer it. It reminds me of something I know I need to know.

FOOTNOTES

1. There are still speakers of Squamish living only a few miles from Bowen Island, with plenty to teach to those who are willing to learn. The best printed source is Aert Kuipers, *The Squamish Language* (The Hague: Mouton, 1967). Hill-Tout had more fluent speakers of Squamish to talk to than Kuipers did, but far less skill at recording what he heard. His *Notes on the sk̓qo'mic of British Columbia* are published in Report 70 of the British Association for the Advancement of Science (London, 1900). This article is partially reprinted in Charles Hill-Tout, *The Salish People*, vol. 2, edited by Ralph Maud (Vancouver: Talonbooks, 1978) — but there the Squamish spellings are haphazardly simplified from Hill-Tout's already dubious versions.
2. Here again the source is Louis Miranda, in conversation with Aert Kuipers.

CHARLOTTE TOWNSEND-GAULT

Charlotte Townsend-Gault has coupled her considerable knowledge of modern art with the study of anthropology in a way that gives her a particularly perceptive view of contemporary aboriginal art. In that field, she was co-curator of *Land, Spirit, Power: First Nations at the National Gallery of Canada,* in 1992 and she is currently working on a major exhibition of paintings and virtual reality displays by (Lawrence Paul) Yuxweluptun for the new Fine Arts Gallery at the University of British Columbia.

Her writing background dates to the late 1960s when she was art critic for *The Vancouver Sun,* and she now contributes regularly to a number of scholarly journals and art magazines, both Canadian and international. This piece is reprinted fom the *American Indian Quarterly* (Vol. #18, No. 4, Fall, 1994) by permission of the University of Nebraska Press.

Townsend-Gault moved with her family to Bowen Island in 1990 because it seemed "as good a place as any from which to pursue a career as an independent curator, editor and writer on contemporary art."

Quite obviously, it was a good decision.

Northwest Coast Art: The Culture of the Land Claims

The cultures of the Northwest Coast have endured against ferocious odds; their continuity is a source of pride. A response to the contemporary art of those cultures must involve a response to their traditions, and the role they play in the lives of the artists. At the same time, the artists must contend with ideas about art, and who and what it is for, that come from completely different sources. To consider the work of the many artists on the Northwest Coast today is to see that, while they share a reverence for those who carved and painted before them, there are important differences in how they articulate what they have learned and in how they have synthesized their sources. What they have in common is that they are part of the culture of the land claims.

For thousands of years, these peoples used the natural abundance of the region to sustain their populations without damaging the forests, without over-fishing the teeming waters, without interfering with the animal populations, without compromising the fertility of the berry bushes and medicinal plants. What is now called "art" was integrated into the whole complex of ways, practical and imaginative, for maintaining a balanced relationship between humans and their environment. While the artistic "tradition" appears to be continuous, the context for it is discontinuous.The importance of the mythologies, the stories that these artists illustrate or draw upon, is not that they are remnants of "the past" in "the present," but that they override the distinction between past and present. In the mythologies of the tribes, from the Tlingit in the north to the Coast Salish in the south, it is clear that humans are not necessarily the main protagonists in the great drama of life, and that humans do not necessarily always triumph. The theme of transformation between the human realm and the realm of animals and spirits, which is the foundation of many stories or family histories, tells of an imaginative closeness between species based on an understanding of the absolute dependency of the human species on the others. This relationship is the basis of the rights in the land that Canada's First Nations claim, as they always have claimed —despite arrangements of a sophistry and duplicity that only colonising self-interests could devise. As a chief expressed it during the Gitksan/Wet'suweten land-claim hearing:

> For us the ownership of territory is a marriage of the Chief and the land. Each Chief has an ancestor who encountered and acknowledged the life of the land. From such encounters came power. The land, the animals and the peoples all have spirit — they all must be shown respect. This is the basis of our law.[1]

As the people recover from the depredations of colonialism, the alien diseases and alien ideologies, all that which enabled strangers to help themselves to their land and its resources, it is their struggle over land claims and rights in the land that is beginning to focus identity. A retreat to the past not being possible, enduring elements are combined with rediscovered and reinvented traditions, with elements of introduced ideologies and new technologies, demonstrating persistent ingenuity and adaptation. The artists in their reach for these recombinant possibilities understand this well. Recent scholarship and cultural productions are further complicating and extending the frame of reference for Northwest Coast art. Marjorie Halpin, a Northwest Coast scholar, has proposed the de-regulation of the style that, since the ethnographer Franz Boas published his highly influential *Primitive Art* (1927), too many have been mislead into reading as codified, but essentially realistic, representations of the natural world. Some social art historians are looking again at the relationship between modern art and its roots in traditions that have been mistakenly labelled "primitive," specifically with reference to the work of Jackson Pollock and Barnett Newman.[2] .

Newman himself acknowledged his own debt to the Northwest Coast where he found a sophisticated abstraction that he tried to emulate. Karen Jamieson's contemporary dance troupe worked on a number of dance performances with the participation and cooperation of many Gitksan people, in which dances were based on some of the Gitksan legends. An opera, *The World is as Sharp as a Knife,* based on the life of Wilson Duff, and growing from an idea of the composer Bruce Ruddell, is in the early production stage. Duff was the anthropologist who, in the 1950s, was largely responsible for the removal of many totem poles from their original sites to the Museum of Anthropology at the University of British Columbia, a move that he later found simultaneously salvaged and destroyed them. It is a story with consequences for the relations between aboriginal populations and colonizing powers that extends far beyond British Columbia.

The pre-history of the Northwest Coast, to which mythology, oral tradition and archaeology contribute, tells of internal migration, contact, conflict and trade reaching back at least 10 thousand years. It also shows the working of stone, and most probably wood, with stone or shell tools. Although the region's high rainfall means that wooden artifacts decay rapidly, petroglyphs survive as do the stone vessels, thought to be ritual tobacco mortars, in which the form of an animal and the form of the bowl are integrated in a way that prefigures the wooden animal-form food vessels that are still made and used today. Copper bracelets and bone combs, dating from 2,500 years ago, covered with finely engraved geometric decoration, have been found in Tsimshian territory. What is now loosely referred to as the Northwest Coast style has long been evolving, adapting to changing circumstances and available materials, as it did so spectacularly with the arrival of metal tools and commercial paint. The re-combinations of change and continuity become evident in considering the art of only a few of the many people working today.

Many artists have been able to learn their skills in the traditional way from an older relative, or from copying, an accepted way of learning long before copying from objects in museums became the only option. Not to be dismissed as "slavish," copying is the best way to get the feel of how the master's chisel, adze or brush had moved. Even among the Haida, with their catastrophic population decline, it has been possible to pick up the threads. As Robert Davidson has said:

> We have many threads connecting us to the past. My grandparents were one of those threads, and when these threads come together they form a thick rope. It is that thick rope that is connecting us to our cultural past, the values which we are reclaiming.[3]

Now, in the 1990s, there is a network of teacher/apprentice relationships, some of them cutting across tribal and stylistic boundaries, as has happened at the Kitanmax School of Northwest Coast Indian Art, part of the 'Ksan Cultural and Educational Centre at Hazelton, founded in 1970. There are now plans, with the new University of Northern British Columbia, to start a school for carvers in Prince Rupert. Many of the younger artists — David Neel, Lawrence Paul, Lyle Wilson, Ron Hamilton — have received part of their training in art schools and universities whose curricula are based on a very different aesthetic history. They fearlessly, if not uncontroversially, are finding ways to blend what they have learned with the aesthetic sensibility that announces them to be Cowichan or Nuu-chah-nulth. Their art cannot be dismissed with terms such as "tradition" and "authenticity" which tend to make a mythologized past into the sole determinant of their artistic activities. They are living in a world where, as Clifford puts it, "the roots of tradition are cut and retied, (and) collective symbols (are) appropriated from external influences."[4]

Among such collective symbols are: the crucifixion, bureaucrats, logging trucks, filing systems, identity cards, oil spills. And among shared, if not always explicit, issues is the challenge to the power structures that came close to bringing these cultures down, that scattered their treasures and controlled how they were represented.

Of the very diverse works produced by these artists over the last two decades, can a generalization be risked? Their work is many things to many people, but it is inescapably part of a current cultural and political effort to protect their environment from further greedy and insensitive inroads, to repatriate their cultural property, to learn everything they can from their elders, to teach their languages to their young. An important part of it is the integration — a political, economic and aesthetic matter simultaneously. This interconnectedness was eloquently expressed by Diane Brown speaking in court for the Haida about herring spawning:

> It's a spiritual thing that happens. It doesn't just happen every year. You can't take that for granted. We can't take that for granted because everything in the environment has to be perfect. The climate has to be perfect. The water temperature. The kelp have to be ready, and the herring have to want to spawn.... But I want to share what goes on in my spiritual self in my body come February.[5]

Logging companies were applying for an injunction to prohibit the Haida from picketing logging roads on Lyell Island in Haida Gwaii. She had requested, and been granted, permission to speak "in the Haida way" about some of the consequences of the proposed interference in the balance of nature, and specifically about the herring spawning, a process with which the consequences of logging can interfere.

It is this widely expressed integration which led Rick Hill, former director of the Insitute of American Indian Art, to venture a defining characteristic: "The interconnectedness of all Indian art is its perimeter of defence."

Artists are heirs to this way of dealing with the world. But they are also part of a society that subscribes to a convention for showing respect to significant works of art, a way of paying careful attention in a controlled setting designed for quiet contemplation and an emphasis on the visual. It is the perceptualism that the art historian Norman Bryson has identified as the defining characteristic of western post-Renaissance art.[6]

If this segregation of art into galleries or museums is the ultimate accolade — conferring the status of art object — it is also the ultimate act of decontextualization, of unconnectedness. Both traditions, both ideas as to what art is and what role it can play, are up for scrutiny in the current social and aesthetic climate. But the traditions are interdependent. The cultural knowledge that governed the making and use of masks and kerfed boxes, and the history that has purloined and labelled them in museum vitrines, are both locked into a present politics of representation.

A central issue in this politics is the question: "Who decides?" What are the forces that determine the significance and value of certain works, and overlook others? It would seem, for example, that overlooking the contribution of women is not the prerogative of any one culture. As Doreen Jensen, Gitksan artist and advocate for the acknowledgement of the contributions of women to the cultures of the Northwest Coast, has pointed out: "There are no divisions amongst our work."[7]

Jensen states, with necessary vehemence, of the baskets, the quill-work boxes, the blankets, that: "The women's work is art, absolutely." If calling the work traditionally done by men "art" is a way of validating it for new audiences, then that which was done by women should also be so validated. The work of a number of Coast Salish women artists in re-establishing the techniques and designs of woven blankets, and renewing the designs in their own versions, is being recognized in this way.

In this "neologistic" cultural politics, tradition is not just a static, a-historical, homogeneous mass waiting to be tapped, but more a contemporary device to make sense of the past, to re-construct and, where necessary, to re-invent it. A blanket by Robin Sparrow, a painting by Doug Cranmer, a screen by Ron Hamilton, a spoon by Robert Davidson, a mask by David Neel are much more than "works of art," no matter how handsome or moving that particular label may make them. The works can be, simultaneously, a synopsis of history, the realization of myth, the revelation of power, the display of prestige, the proof of wealth. Add to this the revision of history and the critique of its representations, and it is apparent that artists, along with native writers, archivists, historians, museum curators — most of whom play more than one role — are re-discovering, adapting, sometimes re-inventing "tradition." The works have a complex range of possible interpretations, purposes and audiences.

Consider some of the other roles played by some of the "visual" artists: Ron Hamilton is a scholar, poet and storyteller; Dorothy Grant, Robert Davidson and Dempsey Bob are dancers; as is Yuxweluptun, a

17

passionate polemicist against the forces that have created our "toxicological environment;" David Neel is a community animator, like Davidson and Grant. They are not the decorators of social events but they contribute the mask, robe or pole that will be integral to the reason for holding the event. Dempsey Bob has no objection to his reputation as a superb bannock-maker, no insignificant skill when you consider that feeding large numbers of people is, with the dancing and display, part of a traditional hospitality that defines the rights and obligations of the participants, performers and spectators.

Dempsey Bob has said: "We come from a society that is very old in art. We have rules within those arts, but you have to know those rules so well that you make them your own."

This is what distinguishes those who use the traditional vocabulary with real authority and daring from the imitators. Bob's daring gives him an indefinable style, proving that individuality and tribal style can co-exist. The Tlingit characteristics in his masks include the flattened squarish face, the prominent ears in the corners, often the combination of two faces in one mask, telling a story, and the sparing use of colour — on mouth, flared nostrils, eyebrows. But there is something more, something as simple as it is awesome. The curves, ogees and ovoids, the elements of mask or panel forming a vibrant mass, are never just that, just elements. They *are* the eye, beak, tail, fin, paw of a specific being; they *are* what they represent. If you go with Dempsey Bob into his workshop in the basement of his house, you see the respect with which he treats the beings that are emerging from the blocks of wood. He keeps each one wrapped up because, as he puts it, "they get at me to finish them all the time." It becomes clear that Bob does not think of himself as making objects so much as locating spirits.

Bob's first instruction came from his grandparents and his mother. He carves all types of wood, designs and engraves jewelry in silver and gold, and works in two-dimensional design, producing drawings, silkscreen prints and button blankets, of which he has designed about 50. His confidence in historical style also gives him the security to incorporate mirrors into his carvings. Playing on the bilateral symmetry that is part of his tradition, the mirrors double a carving and makes the spirit world accessible. Although Dempsey Bob carves for his own people, he also works for a non-native audience. One does not have to know much to know that the suave elegance of his carvings conceals as much as it reveals — what that might be is essentially unknowable to a non-Tlingit audience. Narratives recalling how the spirits were originally revealed to the clan are essential but cannot travel into a collector's home with a carving. Nor can the concept of *at.oow* which is fundamental to Tlingit social structure, oral literature and ceremonial life. *at.oow* cannot readily

18

be translated into English, yet it remains the spiritual, social and rhetorical anchor for oratory, carving and much else.[8] The limit is set not for the sake of mystification, nor is it a hostile withholding for the sake of individual or group power, but its existence acts to protect a cultural power.

Although many would agree with Claude Levi-Strauss' accolade: "I consider that the culture of the Northwest Coast Indians produced an art on a par with that of Greece or Egypt,"[9] it has become too easy for the term "Northwest Coast traditional style" to be misunderstood as stylistic bondage, as suppressing innovation. That artists are not its slaves can be illustrated by the processes through which it has been recovered over the past 30 years. Bill Holm made a great contribution to that recovery by revealing the underlying principles of Northwest Coast idiom in his book *Northwest Coast Art: An Analysis of Form*, first published in 1965. Holm helped to clarify the importance of the formline, ovoid and U-forms, and the intellectual dexterity required to prevent them from becoming formulaic. While many artists count Holm as an important source, one less-satisfactory consequence of his analysis has been the impression that this was an art of limiting factors, consigned to the past.

Understanding the principles is not enough, any more than Angkor Wat or Shakespeare can be understood by consulting a design manual or a grammar book. This is something of the message of Lyle Wilson's print, *Ode to Billy Holm, Lalooska, Duane Pasco and Jonathan Livingstone Seagull* (1980). Wilson has invented a way to represent a figure in motion from the formline vocabulary and in doing so has detached the body from the web of interconnection suggested by the design on the cover of Holm's book which forms the background. The alienated Nuhlmahl figure — it is not clear whether he is a new man or a shadow of his former self — is in search of a new identity against the background of the native ID card, the web of bureaucracy.

A visually powerful idea as to how the great works of the past were constructed has been made possible through the Image Recovery Project, masterminded by Bill McClennan of the Museum of Anthropology at the UBC. Infrared photography has been used to probe painting on boxes and house boards that had all but disappeared under the patina of age and use. It has revealed the artists' breathtaking ingenuity and subtlety in adapting and transposing body parts and characteristics onto a limited space. It also proved that they were not slavish users of templates, for in many cases the symmetry is not exact. These recoveries do much to reanimate the "principles" that have been used in too many of the silkscreen prints produced on the Northwest Coast with trivializing results.

Lyle Wilson is one of the artists who, as part of the Project, has been transposing the recovered images onto new surfaces of wood or paper, an unmatchable way of learning from the past. Speaking of their "painterly nature," Wilson says: "The most revealing aspect of these paintings is the amount of play in which the artist could revel." It is important too that the project "will restore a great deal of humanness and individuality to our present artistic sensibilities."[10]

Although Robert Davidson began carving argillite when very young, it was not until he apprenticed to Bill Reid, who himself had worked to understand and recover Haida carvings from museum collections, that he gained an understanding of the principles that underlay the work of his great-grandfather, the legendary Haida artist Tahayren (Charles Edenshaw). Tahayren's work, in argillite, gold and silver, fortunately endures as one of strongest tangible links with the Haida past. Davidson has devoted himself to an understanding, and hence restitution, of the intellectual terms on which Haida art is built. But this has not been at the expense of the meanings attached to the creatures that appear in his work — the frog, dogfish and eagle among them — that underlay these terms. Early in his career he showed most dramatically how using the "principles" means inventiveness, not stultification. He was one of the first of the new generation to demonstrate that the forms themselves, where line controls space and space solidifies to produce line, where proportion, scale and relationships work together, were capable of infinite, labile inventiveness. Davidson works equally well on monumental scale or small — the silver spoon in which the formlines conform effortlessly to the shape of the spoon is eloquent proof of the intellectual games that Davidson plays with symmetry, which include undoing it. In 1969, Davidson was responsible for the first pole to be raised in his home community of Masset for nearly 90 years. This signalled not only the recovery of old skills but also the recovery of the culture in which important events or the memory of an ancestor were properly marked by a pole.

Originally developed from an ingenious re-thinking of the uses to which silver coins could be put, Haida bracelets continue to play an important role in the potlatch, many families treasuring their horde. In an art that delights in setting puzzles, the jewelry provides a conundrum of its own — is it in two or three dimensions? Davidson's prints and paintings settle this in their own way, but even to the non-Haida it is clear that their two-dimensionality has its origins in something much deeper than is conveyed by the words "pattern" or "design." Formal issues remain at the service of deeper meaning.

Another reminder of the essential role played by women is given in Davidson's tribute to his grandmother, Florence Edenshaw Davidson:

> I have to give Nani a lot of credit for my inspirations. I have a theory
> that the women always kind of kept the art alive because they always

bugged their husbands to do this, do that ... Every time I come home, Nani bugs me about something. 'When will you do my bracelet, when will you do my ring? I need another blanket design.' Every time I come home, she bugs me for a new button blanket design."[11]

In Haida society it is the women who wove the cedar bark or cut and stitched the cloth for the ceremonial robes that display the crests. They were, and still are, "handmade valuables ... ways of recording our history." Dorothy Grant learned to weave spruce root hats and baskets and to work the ceremonial button appliqué robes from Florence Edenshaw Davidson. (Pearl buttons first came to the coast from China as part of the trade in pelts that met the Chinese demand for fur robes.)

Although the collaboration between Davidson and Grant opens up a new range of formal and social possibilities for Haida design, it becomes still clearer that these are not designs stuck on to various media. Grant sees her adaptation of Haida idioms to contemporary fashion garments as part of that "traditional" evolution, not so much a revival of the past as a revival of a culture that was alive and therefore always changing, always evolving, and part of the adaptation to newly available materials. There is a direct line of descent from woven cedar-bark robes to wool, to traded stroud cloth, to felt, to silk. These are grand clothes in any culture, perhaps because they carry with them a Haida idea. As Grant has written:

> By the example our elders have shown us — that appearances are very important in ceremony and self-respect a common value — the way we carry ourselves in public, appearing in a button blanket with our family crest, shows pride in where we come from.[12]

Ron Hamilton is not alone in finding that the restitution of older forms for expressing cultural meaning now has the urgency that formal innovation once possessed. This is no retreat. For artists like Hamilton, adept in many media, the compelling purpose is to clarify and reinvigorate the expressive forms for their contemporaries and for the future — the survival of the language, the stories and their meanings. And he is a spell-binding storyteller who uses his skills as a poet to tell the stories of his people, as well as to express his anguish and his anger.

Hamilton understands that his art, seen in the wider community, undoubtedly serves a public-relations function for his Nuu-chah-nulth culture, but its alienated exhibition is based on a fundamental misunderstanding: "Lately the rule is, 'Don't interpret! It's all art now.' But that's an interpretation, not ours."[13]

Hamilton's superb grasp of the two-dimensional possibilities is perhaps best demonstrated in his large-scale painting of house screens, on both wood and cloth, "art" that remains open to very complex "interpretation." More than a backdrop to dances and ceremonials, these screens acted as announcements about the family, its secular and spiritual status. They also had their own socio-dramatic role to play. Only Hamilton's grasp of the angular clarity of Nuu-chah-nulth design could allow him to deconstruct it, as he does in his print, *Whaling Images* (1977), detaching the components from one another, condensing, stretching and re-assembling in a quadripartite arrangement.

Lyle Wilson and Ron Hamilton have used their skills to work through the apparent conflict between tradition-as-a-constraint and tradition-as-the-basis-for-new-possibilities.

Many artists recognize the danger in the idea that they are bound by tradition. Post-Renaissance Western art history has encouraged the expectation that innovation — change and movement and responsiveness — will be formal and will occur within the frame of the painted rectangle or the three-dimensional mass. On the Northwest Coast not only is there a tradition of change and innovation, but the works, their creation, purpose and eventual destination are inseparable from the artists' often complex social roles. Consider Joe David's large, "traditional" welcome figure, which he made as his ironic contribution to the protest against the logging of Meares Island in Nuu-chah-nulth territory. It became the focus of and symbol for that successful protest. It has a different focus now standing outside the Museum of Anthropology at UBC.

Kwakwaka'wakw art has been able to continue relatively uninterrupted with a line of descent running through the work of revered artists like Charlie James, Mungo Martin, Willie Seaweed and Ellen Neel, the grandmother of David Neel. Ellen Neel was an innovator in as much as she was an important woman artist in the man's world of wood carving, and also because she was the first person, in 1948, to experiment with the printing of design elements from her work on paper and fabric. David Neel understands that his "tradition" has been one of perpetual "innovation." Among the Kwakwaka'wakw precedents for making masks that deal with contemporary social situations and events are starvation masks, smallpox masks, earthquake masks and white man masks. In his turn, Neel has made a group of 20 masks, called *Spirit of the Earth*, some of which have been danced, that personify topical issues such as clearcutting, marine pollution, racism and the pain of relocation for the Inuit. Neel invents new faces and new expressions, and some aspects of each mask pay tribute to the people concerned — Inuit, Tlingit, Rodney King — but his own version of Kwakwaka'wakw style dominates. Neel states: "We are at a point in Canadian history where it is no longer as easy for government bureaucrats to suppress the needs of the first citizens."[14]

Just Say No commemorates a momentous event in reaching this point. Elijah Harper, New Democratic Party member of the Manitoba legislature, indicated his "No" to the proposed Meech Lake accord, which was about to overlook the needs of the First Nations, with a gesture of an eagle feather. By transforming native values into collective symbols for the society at large, Neel's interpretation of this moment makes clear that it was not obstructive but constructive — the copper, always representative of wealth for Kwakwaka'wakw, here represents the wealth of the Canadian nation, while there is a canoe paddle for each province. As Neel puts it: "In paddling a canoe the paddlers all work together, as it must be with a country."

Two Northwest Coast artists, Don Yeomans and Wayne Alfred, have made another syncretic symbol by giving the crucifixion a new range of meaning. Yeomans' *Raven on a Cross* is open to at least two potentially contradictory readings. One is the usurping of one culture's way of explaining the mysteries of the universe by another culture. The other is the alliance of those cultures. Yeomans has produced the unforgettable image of Raven, the proud and subtle cultural hero, pinioned to the cross. Raven, in some of his guises at least, is a saviour to the people. Christianity, with its central theme of the crucified saviour, was, and remains, widely accepted by many people on the Northwest Coast; it offered solace in a time of catastrophic upheaval in their way of life, even as it usurped and contributed to the destruction of indigenous forms of spirituality. Over time it has become clearer where Christian doctrine is close to native thought — and where it sharply diverges. Missionary-run residential schools, in trying to instil their own code of ethics, took away the language, often brutally, and failed to understand the complex ethical code which it expressed. At the same time, the suffering of the saviour provided an example for the suffering of his new followers. In 1922, the *Indian Act of 1884* was amended to outlaw the potlatch and other ceremonies through which the succession of chiefs was validated and the transfer of cultural property and territory collectively acknowledged. Totem poles and masks were destroyed or forcibly removed, a situation which these artists of the land claims are trying to rectify.

Another crucifixion, Wayne Alfred's *Golgotha,* is disturbing on a visceral level. It, too, surprises by handling the subject matter of one art history in the manner of another to convey a personal blend of beliefs. Alfred's treatment of the suffering of a native Christ seems to authorize the use of a term borrowed from western art history: Baroque. It draws on the fearfulness of death and comes close to overstating it. It is the death's head underneath the cross that is dominant, just as the lowest figure on the totem pole is the most significant.

During his education at the Emily Carr College of Art and Design in Vancouver, Yuxweluptun (Lawrence Paul, he regards as his "white man's alias"), was exposed to ideas about colour, space and form from a tradition far removed from the Northwest Coast. In a deliberate act of reciprocal appropriation, he has integrated these ideas into his work to create an idiom as hybrid as any in western 20th-century art. Yuxweluptun's painting has taken two principal and inter-related directions over the past decade. In one, he has staked out a space within contemporary art discourse wherein the idioms and evolutionary principles of his own Cowichan culture can be a serious and inevitable vehicle for contemporary thought and social enquiry. Simultaneously, Yuxweluptun's social concerns have come increasingly to focus on the environment, especially the effects of mining, clear-cutting and other intrusions into his land. He continues to produce the large canvases refining the synthetic idiom evident in such significant pieces as *Protector* (1991) and *Red Man Watching White Man Trying to Fix Hole in Sky* (1990). At the same time his first experiment with virtual reality enables the viewer to "enter" a Longhouse and "move around" within it while watching the Spirit Dancing. In the large (124.24 x 226.06 cm) painting, *Red Man Watching White Man Trying to Fix Hole in Sky,* the "red man" is positioned according to post-Renaissance conventions for rendering the "figure in the landscape," but he is assembled, in three-dimensional space, from generic Northwest Coast formlines and ovoids. This makes him skeletal, a hollow man, yet he is conjoined with his mask. His face is a mask, the mask his face, and this mask is specific to the Cowichan band where Yuxweluptun is a spirit dancer. In this characteristic work, Yuxweluptun, who now lives near the world's largest clearcut in northern British Columbia, appropriates figural and landscape conventions from the western art tradition, to picture what he calls "our toxicological environment." This condition has been brought about, in his words, by the "European ethos — your utilitarian, imperious, imperialistic power and your capitalistic value of authoritarianism" which has "destroyed First Nations' ancestral sacred lands in fewer than five hundred years."[15]

Faced with a situation of dangerous absurdity, Yuxweluptun himself has always shown an affinity with aspects of surrealism, and his work is full of quotations from its oleaginous style. But his impetus is not personal analysis — as he points out, "Dali wasn't doing salvation art."

In both painting and virtual reality, Yuxweluptun has developed a taxonomy of great pictorial inventiveness and moral seriousness. In analyzing the inter-relationship between pollution and power, scrutinizing its effects and deliberating solutions, he has displaced "landscape" and reinstated a spirit world. The conclusion must be that the opposition between nature and culture was always a fallacy, and that forces us to reconsider our response to the issues.

In looking at its contemporary art, it becomes clear that there is no single story line for the Northwest Coast, and that, in spite of a certain mythic quality that it has acquired in the telling, there never has been.

Also clear is the strong sense of historical continuity and an even stronger sense of the artists working to discover more about it. An important part of that discovery is done by looking and feeling. At the same time, they are taking their place in that part of the contemporary art discourse which gives art a critical role — critical both of itself and its social context. It is a critique which, in the case of Hamilton and some others, extends to withdrawing their work from public view, where this move makes a statement as significant as the public advocacy found in Yuxweluptun and Neel, or the dramatization of ideological conflict found in Alfred's *Golgotha* and Yeoman's *Raven on a Cross* or the extensions of a brilliant melding of form and meaning in Grant and Davidson.

Such a list illustrates the diversity of ways in which Northwest Coast artists retain the interconnectedness of their traditions. They are using their own work as a mode of enquiry that can scrutinize itself, that can self-consciously announce its power, and, as well, engage with its much older sources of power.

FOOTNOTES

1. Gitksan chief quoted in Knudsen, Peter and David Suzuki. *Wisdom of the Elders.* 1992. (Toronto: Stoddart) p. 128.,

2. See for example, Jackson Rushing, *The Impact of Nietzche and Northwest Coast Indian Art on Barnett Newman's idea of Redemption and the Abstract Sublime.* 1988. *Art Journal,* Vol. 47. pp. 187-195.

3. Robert Davidson, Presentation to a Public Meeting, Masset, Haida Gwaii, July 7, 1991, p. 6.

4. Clifford, James. 1988. *The Predicament of Culture: Twentieth Century Ethnography, Literature and Art.* (Cambridge, Mass.: Harvard University Press) p. 15.

5. Norbert Ruebsaat, "Speaking with Diane Brown", *Borderlines,* #16, Fall 1989, pp. 18-23. Testimony given by Diane Brown before Mr. Justice Harry MacKay in the B.C. Supreme Court on November 6th, 1985.

6. Bryson, Norma, 1983, *Logic of the Gaze.* (New Haven and London: Yale University Press).

7. Doreen Jensen, author of *Robes of Power: Totem Poles on Cloth,* 1986, (Vancouver: University of British Columbia Press) in conversation with the curators of *Land, Spirit, Power,* August, 1991.

8. The concept of *at.oow* is discussed at length in Dauenhauer, Nora Marks and Richard Dauenhauer, *Haa Shuka: Our Ancestors — Tlingit Oral Narratives,* 1987, (Juneau: Sealaska Heritage Foundation). This book, with its companion volume, *Haa Tuwunaagu Yis, for Healing Our Spirit: Tlingit Oratory,* 1990, are anthologies of the oratory, given in two languages, with glossary and commentary.

9. Claude Levi-Strauss in *Time* magazine at the opening of the exhibition, *Masterworks of Canadian Indian and Eskimo Art,* in Paris, 1967, quoted in Geeorge MacDonald, *Prehistoric Art of the Northern Northwest Coast,* 1976, ed. Roy L. Carlson. (Burnaby, B.C.: Dept. of Archaeology, Simon Fraser University) p. 99.

10. Lyle Wilson quotations are taken from texts accompanying the exhibition, *The Image Recovery Project,* at the Museum of Anthropology, University of British Columbia, 1992.

11. Davidson's remarks, made in August 1978, are quoted in Margaret B. Blackman, *During My Time: Florence Edenshaw Davidson, A Haida Woman,* 1982, (Seattle: University of Washington Press, Vancouver and Toronto: Douglas and McIntyre) p. 124.

12. Dorothy Grant, "Sculpting on Cloth" in *Robes of Power: Totem Poles on Cloth,* 1986, Doreen Jensen and Polly Sargent, eds. (Vancouver: University of British Columbia Press). p.60.

13. Ron Hamilton, *Box of Darkness* in B.C. Studies, special issue, *In Celebration of our Survival: The First Nations of British Columbia.* No. 89,

Spring 1991, Doreen Jensen and Cheryl Brooks, eds. (Vancouver: University of British Columbia Press) p. 62.

14. B.C. Studies, special issue *In Celebration of Our Survival: The First Nations of British Columbia*, No. 89, Spring 1991. Doreen Jensen and Cheryl Brooks, eds. (Vancouver: University of British Columbia Press) p.138.

15. Lawrence Paul, *Red Savages Meet Tight Pink-Skinned Men: 1492-1992*, in *Indigena: Contemporary Native Perspectives.* p.158.

Victor Chan

Victor is a typical Bowen Islander: a particle physicist and restaurateur, who writes colossal travel guides in his spare time. In truth, he is in every way a-typical, or more correctly, exceptional. Born in Hong Kong and educated in Canada and the United States, Victor was doing graduate work in the dank corridors of the Enrico Fermi Institute at the University of Chicago when he realized that the secrets of life would not be solved by smashing muons. He set out on a world journey that took him, by chance, to Dharamsala, where he met the Dalai Lama. That spawned a fascination with Tibet that was only heightened by the mysterious beauty of the Himalayas. Through persistent study and personal pilgrimage, unprecedented by a Westerner, he came up with the material for his recent 1,100-page *Tibet Handbook: A Pilgrimage Guide,* published by Moon Publications of San Francisco, from which this section is excerpted. Victor moved to Bowen more than a year ago and now runs the Bowen Island Cafe with his East German wife Susanne and their year-old daughter Lina.

Tibetan Concepts
of Pilgrimage

All mountains, all rivers, holy lakes, tirthas (places of pilgrimage), the
abodes of seers, cow-pens, and temples of gods are sin-destroying localities.
— Sakyamuni

Mythic Origins of Pilgrimage Sites

Just before Buddha died, he designated four places that should
inspire his followers: Lumbini, his place of birth; Bodh Gaya, where he
attained enlightenment; Sarnath, where he gave his first sermon; and
Kashinagara, where he died. These places, all in India except for
Lumbini, became the four greatest pilgrimage sites of Buddhism. The
most important is Bodh Gaya, regarded as the "diamond seat" of enlightenment for all Buddhas, and thus the spiritual centre of the universe.

In Hindu mythology, pilgrimage sites represent places, known as
pitha, where parts of the body of the mother goddess (*Sati*) fell to earth.
In Tibetan Tantric Buddhism, the soil of India is venerated as the spiritual body of the Buddha, divided into 24 parts, corresponding to 24
famous holy places in northeast India. Tibetans have duplicated them by
taking their relics to specific places within Tibet and building shrines to
house them. For example, Pabonka Monastery on the outskirts of Lhasa
is said to be a replica of Devikota, a temple in Gauhati (*Assam*), which in
turn was based on Kushinagara, the place of Buddha's death. There are at
least three copies of Devikota in Tibet; each was consecrated with a piece

of rock from Devikota itself. These 24 geographical pilgrimage places constitute an outer (*chi*), visible series of sacred sites. The inner (*nang*) series is located within one's own body, providing specific centres for the process of meditation. Lastly, there are 24 symbolic spheres of the mandala, which constitute the secret (*sang*) division.

How a Site Came to Be Sanctified

GEOMANTIC ATTRIBUTES

Geomancy, or the art of divination by means of geographical features, plays a vital role in determining Tibet's pilgrimage places. The sanctity of a site is largely derived from its special natural and physical attributes, rather than from the shrine erected there. The image consecrated in a monastery is, of course, important and pilgrims have a natural wish to pay homage to it. However, for the most significant sites, it is the geomantic and metaphysical character of the place that makes it worthy of worship.

Certain naturally occurring pilgrimage sites (caves, rivers, mountains, lakes, river sources) are endowed with subtle and ineffable powers that can trigger unusual responses from pilgrims. There is a widespread Tibetan belief that they are the abodes of local deities capable of helping or harming pilgrims who propitiate these deities by making regular offerings. Mountains are particularly important. In ancient myths, heavenly beings used them as vehicles to enter this world. Seven of Tibet's early kings descended to earth via sacred mountains. These personify the soul (*la*) of the communities that worship them as ancestral deities. This soul could be physically represented not only by a mountain (*lari*) but by a lake (*latso*); the former takes on a male aspect, the latter female. The soul or "life-spirit" of Tibet is associated with Lhamo Latso — "Soul-lake of the Goddess" — (the goddess in this case is Palden Lhamo, Protectress of Tibet). The soul of an individual, on the other hand, may reside in a tree (*lashing*) or in a turquoise (*layü*) worn around the neck. Tibetans take particular care to maintain the well-being of the collective or individual souls by means of offerings. In the event of calamities brought on by the "loss of soul", the ritual of lakhug — the retrieval of the soul — is performed.

ASSOCIATION WITH PAST MASTERS AND HISTORICAL FIGURES

Important pilgrim sites are often closely connected with the lives of saints, ascetics, and important historical figures. In many cases, these shrines began as simple retreat caves or hermitages inhabited by renowned yogins. The most important places frequented by the Buddha in his travels and used for meditation by Guru Rinpoche (*Padmasambhava*), the Indian tantric master who first introduced Buddhism into Tibet in the 8th century. Most of the latter are located in hard-to-reach places, at the top of isolated valleys or near the summit of mountains. Many of Guru Rinpoche's caves are at the centre of a geographic mandala that has powerful geomantic attributes. Like many of Tibet's earliest temples, they often face eastwards. Milarepa, the beloved poet-saint of the 11th century, is another celebrated master who consecrated many cave retreats in his lifetime. The most famous of these can be found in the Lapchi area and the Kyirong Valley. Temples built by the first Buddhist king, Songsten Gampo, and his consorts, are also highly sanctified places of pilgrimage.

THE CONSECRATION OF A SITE BY SACRED OBJECTS

The pilgrimage sites were often consecrated when they became repositories for sacred objects. These fall broadly into three categories:

1) Kuten — images of the Buddha and other divinities, symbolizing the sacred body (*ku*);

2) Sungten — sacred books, representing the sacred speech (*sung*);

3) Thugten — chörtens, symbolizing the sacred thought (*thug*).

Chörtens are monuments that hold the relics of important religious personages — a tradition passed down since the time of the Buddha himself. His relics were kept in various places, which became major pilgrimage sites for all Buddhists. The practice of keeping and perhaps displaying the relics of a holy person is quintessentially Buddhist and does not derive from any known Hindu precedent.

Chörtens may be built to commemorate some noteworthy activity of a holy person. This may be the place where he experienced a profound insight or where he was ordained. Sometimes certain highly blessed chörtens can be classified as *thongdröl* — "Liberation on Sight." Before its near-total destruction in the 1960s, the Jampaling chörten in the Dranang Valley was considered such a monument. It was thought to have the power to enlighten any true believer who had the good fortune to set eyes on it.

Thus a pilgrimage can be made to a monastery housing a statue of the Jowo (*Sakyamuni*) or to a chörten that contains the relics of a saint. Tibet's most famous shrine, the Jokhang of Lhasa, used to contain an abundance of these three classes of sacred relics. During the Cultural Revolution, most were plundered or destroyed by the Red guards. Its principal image, Jowo, which confers immense spiritual power on the temple, somehow survived. In recent years, many new statues have been erected and consecrated; the Jokhang is slowly taking on new life.

31

It should be noted that a statue, chörten, or any religious object made by man has no liturgical properties unless it has been sanctified in a consecration ceremony known as rabne. When this occurs, life-force is imbued into the object, usually by means of the sogshing (life-tree). In statues, this takes the form of a blessed wooden stick, inscribed with prayers or mantras, placed inside the body.

SOME SPECIAL CHARACTERISTICS OF SACRED OBJECTS

Quite often, Tibetans attach a miraculous quality to a particular image or object. For example, a Drölma statue might be known as a Drölma Sungjöma — the "Talking Tara" — if legends tell of it having spoken aloud at some early time; to give admonishments or predictions. Another class of well-known miraculous objects are the stones whose surfaces are ostensibly imprinted with the hand or footprints of a master. These relics are highly venerated in monasteries, sometimes transcending other conventional religious objects. In Bodh Gaya, the Buddha's footprint is over 60 cm long. A third attribute is rangjung ("self-manifestation"). Tibetans believe that an object can be formed supernaturally by itself, with no apparent intervention by man. Certain revered statues are considered rangjung, having come into being miraculously — crystallizations of a mystic process. Pilgrims believe that these objects are endowed with special power; they make a special point of viewing and touching them with their foreheads. Sometimes, they are said to dispense holy liquid or ambrosia (*dutsi*) to the worthy, usually through their finger tips.

Motivations of Pilgrimage

The overriding purpose of pilgrimage is the desire to benefit mankind. Most authentic pilgrims make offerings and prayers so that their fellow beings may share the merits gained from the pilgrimage. However, personal gains, both spiritual and material, are also motives for the trip. It is hoped that by undertaking an arduous journey, for example, the sins accrued in the past might be wiped out, religious consciousness expanded. This would promote a better rebirth during the next lifetime, so that the privations of the present life may be exchanged for a better future. The attainment of physical well-being is another common desire. Some women go on pilgrimage with the hope of begetting an offspring. Perhaps the most common wish is simply to have personal contact with the icon or divine objects at the end of the journey. This may be a face-to-face encounter with the Jowo of the Jokhang in Lhasa or a successful circumambulation of the sacred Mount Kailash.

The pilgrimage experience is highly subjective. Pilgrims through the ages have reported their own personal visions of events experienced. Quite a few tell of how they heard the strains of divine music in the depths of lakes, and some recount sighting mythical creatures coming out of the water. These supernatural encounters are likely to be triggered by the heightened spirituality of the pilgrimage experience. The varieties of religious experience described by different persons performing the same journey can be rather surprising.

Casual pilgrims only travel for a limited time. They tend to imitate the behaviour of a sannyasi (one who has taken the vows of abandonment and who formally renounces all earthly ties, embracing the pilgrimage discipline full time in order to seek enlightenment) in regard to dress, food restrictions, and behaviour. Through this they gain true insight and deepen their understanding of the pilgrimage process. At the end of the day, they may sense that they have achieved something meaningful. Indeed, for some, the result may be so rewarding that they become full-time pilgrims.

The Buddhist Idea of Paradise

Inherent in naturally sanctified sites are the ideals of paradise. The entry into a Buddhist paradise is the same as attaining nirvana — the final liberation from the never-ending cycle of rebirth and suffering. The most popular is Sukhavati, the mythical "Western Paradise" of the Buddha Amitabha (*Wöpame*). According to a Tibetan text, this fabulous retreat is full of wish-fulfilling trees, where no wish is denied. There is no suffering or sorrow; the finest silk, food, and precious stones are there for the taking. Caves have springs where milk flows perpetually, lakes bestow clarity of mind, and certain caves promote full enlightenment. While here, the bodhicitta ("Buddha mind") of a pilgrim increases and ignorance is wiped out. The admission into Sukhavati has one proviso: once entered, it can never be left, for the return route is impossible to find.

According to Tibetan pilgrimage literature, there are a number of paradisiacal sites already in existence in Tibet. Some have long been "opened" by appropriate masters but others still await discovery. Dremojong and Chörten Nyima on the Tibet-Sikkim border, Khembalung in Nepal, Lapchi and Rongshar on the Nepal-Tibet border, and the Pemakö Valley in southeast Tibet are probably the best-known "hidden valleys" (*beyuls*). It is widely believed that when wars and other calamities threaten the very survival of mankind, these special places will serve as refuge for the followers of Buddhism.

To gain entry to an "opened" beyul, the pilgrim must first possess profound faith that the beyul actually exists. Secondly, he must have accumulated much merit in his lifetime and be completely detached from worldly goods and desires. Finally, the pilgrim must have access to the proper guidebook and the timing has to be right. Usually this knowledge of a specified date of entry is passed from guru to disciple by secret oral transmission. The approach on foot has to be from one of the pre-ordained cardinal points, depending on the time of the year. In order to reach Dremojong in autumn, for example, it is necessary to use the east gate.

One of the best-known mythical earthly paradises is Shambala. Although much has been written about it in Tibetan sacred literature, no one has been able to pinpoint exactly the whereabouts of this hidden kingdom. Texts that describe the routes to the site underline the fact that only accomplished yogins, steeped in the practice of meditation and spiritual transformation, can possibly overcome the supernatural obstacles along the way. Shambala is one of five major Buddhist pilgrimage sites situated at the cardinal points of the compass. Bodh Gaya is at the centre. Wutai Shan is to the east, Potala (not to be confused with Lhasa's Potala), in the south, Uddiyana in the west, and Shambala in the north.

Devotional Acts of Pilgrims

In order to gain access to a paradisiacal inner sanctum — the final goal of many pilgrimages — pilgrims first must purify themselves, make appropriate offerings, and pass a series of tests that may have both physical and mental components. Dangerous situations, such as negotiating a precipitous catwalk to reach the inner recesses of a cave, test the concentration of the pilgrim's mind. These procedures ensure a level of spirituality sufficient to identify and worship the mythical objects that a nonbeliever cannot see. A simple cave near the top of a ridge may possess extraordinarily potential power, fully charged with the vibrations of great yogis. An indistinct outline on a rock face may manifest a clear image of Chenresi, the Bodhisattva of Compassion, to the pious. The ability to discern the supernatural is considered a vital sign of a pilgrim's progress. It is a measure of transcendental awareness; a significant increase in merit. Those who have it may follow in the footsteps of past masters, who were usually depicted as humble persons, succeeding against all odds in reaching the promised land. The most important religious observances of a pilgrim visiting sacred sites are as follows:

CIRCUMAMBULATION

"Pilgrimage" in Tibetan is *nekhor*, which literally means "the circumambulation of a sacred place." The practice was derived from

Buddhist India, where it began as a means of paying homage to a sacred person or object. The holy site can be a monastery, lake, mountain (in particular Mount Kailash), chörten, or tree. The act of walking clockwise around it, usually many times and accompanied by prayers, is a show of devotion and a means of acquiring merit. It also helps one to be spiritually centred. In India (especially in the south) as well as in Tibet, temples still have corridors (*khorlam*) designed specifically for this purpose. Some good examples are at the Jokhang in Lhasa and at Shalu Monastery.

PROSTRATION

Prostration (*chaktshal*) is a predominantly Tibetan tradition. To show his faith, the pilgrim stretches himself fully on the ground and his progress around the circuit is measured in repetitions of this arduous performance. Usually, every time a pilgrim enters a monastery, he prostrates three times as a matter of course. In each instance, his folded hands touch his forehead, the mouth-throat area, and his heart. This three-pointed contact symbolizes mind, speech and body.

MANTRAS

Mantras are not to be equated with the prayers that often accompany the act of offering. They are formulae used by pilgrims to achieve a meditative state and are usually recited during a journey from sacred site to sacred site. Mantras are considered to be imbued with magic and their incantation supposedly produces supernatural results. For example, the recitation of certain mantra in a certain site can help cure blindness. The Shara Bumpa chörten in the Phanyul Valley is such a monument.

In Tibet, the most ubiquitous mantra is "Om Mani Padme Hum." The verbal symbol of Chenresi, the Bodhisattva of Compassion and the protector of Tibet, it is often seen carved on stones and large rocks. Guru Rinpoche's mantra is "Om Ah Hum Vajra Guru Padme Siddhi Hum." Pilgrims believe the blessing of this supreme master will be conferred on those who recite it. Thousands of powerful mantras are printed on prayer flags (*lungta*). Likewise, the interior of properly consecrated images contains numerous mantras.

Very often a Tibetan performs three prostrations in front of an image, or recites a mantra three times. The first performance prevents the practitioner from falling into the lower realms of existence (*nyensong*); the second helps the person to attain a higher level of rebirth; and the third helps to sublimate negative feelings like anger and hatred.

OFFERINGS

Tibetans on pilgrimage regularly make offerings (*chöpa*) to express thanks and obeisance to the divinities within monasteries or natural places. This gesture, one of the most important for the pilgrim, allows him to propitiate the deities and in doing so ask that particular wishes be granted. By making offerings regularly, the pilgrim knows that he is also accumulating merit for the future.

The object most frequently used in offering is the ceremonial scarf (*khata*), which is usually draped around the neck of a statue or a lama. Others include the five grains, butter lamps (*marme*), and barley beer (*chang*). The last is traditionally offered to shrines associated with Guru Rinpoche and Palden Lhamo, the female divinity. One type of tribute derived from pre-Buddhist practices incense (*sang*); fragrant juniper is burned at sacred sites and on top of passes or mountains. The way in which the smoke rises indicates good or bad omens.

Fundamentally, the concept of offerings implies giving (*jinpa*); it becomes a path to knowledge, fulfilment, peace, and other desired qualities. The most extreme form is to give one's life. One necessary condition for the art of giving, however, is that the pilgrim must do so of his own volition with no thought of reward. The other is compassion. An interesting practice of the Tibetans is the purchase from the butcher of condemned animals. After the transaction, the animal, usually a goat or a sheep, is then set free and allowed to live out its days.

Another simple practice of giving can be seen on mountain tops or passes. The pilgrim who finally reaches the summit puts one stone on top of a cairn (*lhatse*), which in turn is formed of the efforts of many a bygone pilgrim. This is known as the "eye-viewed" offering (*chezing*). The stone cairns allow travellers to see the tops of passes, even from afar, and they provide necessary landmarks for a journey. The offering of a prayer flag on a pass is for the same motive.

Ritual Water Splashing

Tibetans, unlike Hindus, have no tradition of purifying themselves by immersion in sanctified water such as the Ganges. For the Hindus, this is one of the most notable ways of expressing devotion. Water is an important element of purification in Tibetan Buddhism, but it is abstracted. This is well illustrated at the glacial lake called Thukje Dzingbu ("Lake of Compassion"), or Gourikund, on the Mount Kailash circumambulation circuit. While Hindus plunge themselves into the icy water, Tibetans merely splash a few drops in all directions and on their heads. There is a Tibetan saying: "Hindus clean outside, Tibetans clean inside."

Lakes and rivers are important centres of pilgrimage. A good example is the Oracle Lake of Tibet, known as Lhamo Latso. In order to divine their past and future, the Dalai Lamas were obliged to visit it at least once in their lives. Some sacred lakes are associated with the birth of important saints: Guru Rinpoche is said to have been born from a lotus in a lake called Pema Tso. The source of the Indus, a short distance north of Mount Kailash, is a place of veneration for Tibetan pilgrims.

AUDIENCE

One primary aspect of pilgrimage is to obtain an audience (*darsan*) with the lama or guru of a sanctuary. Quite often, the spirituality of a place is derived from the person who stays there. Lapchi is one of the most important pilgrimages in Tibet because Milarepa lived and died there. Dharamsala, which three decades ago had no religious significance whatsoever, is now one of the major centres for pilgrims simply by virtue of the Dalai Lama's presence.

Affiliated with the concept of darsan is the practice of blessing (*jin-lab*). This is usually a touch on the head by the lama, a gift of an offering cake (*torma*); or the bestowing of a blessed knotted string or cloth (*sung-dud*), usually red or yellow, to be worn around the neck. It is believed that a sacred person has the power to consecrate by touch. He can transfer this blessing into an object by blowing on it and reciting a mantra. Perfected medicine (*mandrub*) is another highly prized substance. These small granules are usually dispensed by the lama with a tiny silver spoon and are received with immense care and appreciation. They are believed to possess supernatural curative powers and may save lives during an emergency.

Tantric Pilgrimage

Pilgrimage for the believer is a conscious choice rather than an onerous duty. It need not necessarily conform to a fixed, rigidly prescribed itinerary. There are also no specific ceremonies to be performed in any one place. Taking this idea of the unstructured journey further, it is feasible for a pilgrimage to be internalized. The entire journey is visualized in the mind's eye, thus eliminating the need for an actual voyage.

The basis of a Tantric Pilgrimage is to correlate the outer, geographical sites with the inner regions or organs in the body of the practitioner. For example, the spinal column is imagined to be Mount Meru, the four limbs to be the four mystic subcontinents around it. Actual physical pilgrimage is thus not an absolute requirement in the search for enlightenment. It is eminently possible to realize ultimate emancipation without ever setting foot in any shrines or walking any pilgrimage routes.

NEIL BOYD

Neil Boyd was an undergraduate student, studying psychology at the University of Western Ontario, when he began to notice what he calls "the lack of fit between reality and public policy" in the area of legal and illegal drugs. He has maintained an interest in the subject ever since, both during his graduate studies at Osgoode Hall in Toronto (LL.B., LL.M.) and during his subsequent career at Simon Fraser University, where he is now the director of the School of Criminology. This article stands as the introductory chapter to his recent book, *High Society: Legal and Illegal Drugs in Canada* (Key Porter).

He has published three other books, *The Social Dimensions of Law* and *The Last Dance: Murder in Canada* (both with Prentice Hall) and *Canadian Law: An Introduction* (Harcourt Brace). A fifth book, *Desire and Violence* (Little Brown) is due out soon. He has also produced three television documentaries for the Knowledge Network, two on drugs and one on murder, and is frequently consulted as an analyst by other media.

He and his wife Isabel Otter were at the cutting edge of the modern migration when they moved to Bowen Island in 1979. "It was just hippies and rednecks, then," he says. It would take another book to debate how it has changed, and whether that's a good thing.

Can We
Just Say No
to a War
Against Drugs?

Human beings have been using drugs for thousands of years, eating opium and marijuana, chewing the coca leaf, consuming the potions of various "medicine men," drinking alcohol and inhaling tobacco smoke. There is no culture on earth that has abstained from intoxicants, with the possible exception of the Inuit. Unable to grow the plants that produce drugs, the people of the Arctic Circle had to wait until we brought them alcohol, tobacco and the others.

We take drugs to provide pleasure, to relieve pain, to increase productivity, to alter mood and very occasionally, to allow for the possibility of spiritual or emotional insight. We drink our morning coffee, a little kickstart for the morning rush hour. We light our cigarettes, the relaxing complement to our stimulants. And, later in the day, maybe at lunch and probably at dinner, we drink a little or a lot of alcohol.

We are a country of drug takers. About 80 per cent of adult Canadians drink alcohol, about 70 per cent drink coffee and about 30 per cent smoke tobacco. About 10 per cent of us, mostly women, are prescribed tranquillizers, and about 10 per cent smoke marijuana. Cocaine is used by about two per cent of Canadians; amphetamines, hallucinogens and opiates are regularly consumed by less than one per cent of the population.

These patterns of use vary as we travel around the globe. In most countries, coffee, tobacco, marijuana and opium are, in that order, the most popular of mind-active drugs. In most of the Persian Gulf, alcohol is the least culturally acceptable of consciousness-altering experiences, the subject of Islamic prohibition. In Japan, tobacco consumption is almost twice as popular as it is in Canada, marijuana use is relatively rare and intravenous use of amphetamines is significant, accounting for more than 50,000 criminal-court appearances each year. Almost half of those in Japanese jails are serving time for amphetamine offences. Almost 50 per cent of French women and almost 20 per cent of French men are prescribed tranquillizers and other sedatives for use on a daily basis. The French also drink about twice as much alcohol per capita as Canadians or Americans and slightly more than most of their European neighbours; they are the world's most practised consumers of wine.

Drug use and drug control vary across time and geography, products of specific nations and communities operating in specific historical contexts. "The drug problem" is usually conceived by government and industry as a blend of public-health and criminal enforcement, but it is rarely understood as a cultural phenomenon.

However, similar drugs have different meanings in different cultures. What a drug actually does to you isn't nearly as important as the social context in which it is used and distributed. In many parts of 16th-century Europe, after the introduction of tobacco from the New World, tobacco users and distributors were imprisoned and even executed. In 17th-century Europe, shortly after the introduction of coffee, the Catholic church forbade its consumption, promoting wine as a more appropriate sacrament. Over the last 1,000 years of human history, at different times and in different places, tobacco, caffeine, alcohol, marijuana, cocaine and opium have all been prohibited, and their users and distributors tortured, imprisoned or executed.

In the current era, cultural scripts have also taken precedence over public-health concerns. While marijuana is a less toxic drug than either tobacco or alcohol, its consumption in Western industrial culture has been tied to dissident youth and a rejection of dominant values. Although amphetamines are more potent stimulants than cocaine and have longer-lasting effects, they are not the object of criminal prohibition. Amphetamines are produced by First World pharmaceutical companies, cocaine by the Indians of various South American mountain ranges.

I first learned of the significance of cultural context in Grade 8. My entry in the local Legion's public-speaking contest the previous year was a stirring tribute to Winston Churchill, and had been enthusiastically received. In my senior year of elementary school I decided to deliver a speech entitled "LSD — The Potential Medical and Social Benefits."

It was not well received. In 1965, LSD was virtually unknown, at least in my small town of Deep River, Ontario, but the concept of profoundly altering consciousness was disturbing to the Legionnaires and others. And the suggestion that this drug might be usefully integrated into our culture was threatening, even coming from a 13-year-old boy who hadn't the faintest idea what he was talking about.

Taking issue with these cultural norms as an adult can also be seen as an act of economic and political heresy. *Out of Control* was a documentary about drugs, prepared in 1990 for the CTV national network by Stornoway Productions, a Toronto-based company with a reputation for thoughtful work on complex political issues. The documentary was a substantial commitment, signed by outgoing CTV president Murray Chercover as one of his last decisions before his departure. *Out of Control* was to be two hours in length and to air in prime time, with a budget of several hundred thousand dollars. I was hired by Stornoway to arrange and assist with interviews with convicted drug dealers, and to be interviewed for the program.

When a rough cut of *Out of Control* was shown to the new directors of the network, including president John Cassaday, they had few concerns about the production values, but a lot to say about the message. Illegal drug dealers and drug users, informers and police had not been portrayed as they had wanted them to be. My appearance had not helped. I had argued that the real drug pushers are not those who sell illegal drugs, but those who have the right to advertise their drugs, the purveyors of alcohol and tobacco.

In retrospect, it was probably not surprising that John Cassaday would have found this premise upsetting. Between 1972 and 1976, he had worked in marketing and sales promotion for the Canadian subsidiary of the RJR-Macdonald tobacco company, selling what he likely believed was a legitimate commodity rather than a dangerous drug.

The final product was cut to one hour and rightly criticized in the media for its "trite conclusions" and "predictable images." The original rough cut had not advocated the legalization of drugs, or anything else particularly extreme. It had, however, presented differing points of view on drug control and some of the quirky contradictions of the business. The mistake that the filmmakers made was to believe that they could discuss legal drugs like tobacco and alcohol with the illegal drugs — marijuana, cocaine and heroin.

That is not to say that most drugs are pharmacologically similar or that they pose similar physical and social risks. There are profound and important public-health differences, but they are overshadowed by cultural beliefs and by existing forms of social and economic organization. The legality or illegality of drugs has shaped the way in which we understand pharmacological consequences. Tobacco, alcohol and pharmaceuticals are all billion-dollar industries, approved by the state and occasional-

41

ly subsidized. Heroin, cocaine and marijuana are also billion-dollar industries, prohibited by the state; the eradication of these industries has consistently been subsidized.

Tobacco, for example, is a multi-billion-dollar revenue producer for government and the industry. The drug rose to prominence in Canada during the 1920s with mechanization and cigarette-package production. Before 1920, tobacco was consumed more sporadically, smoked in pipes, cigars and hand-rolled cigarettes.

Opium, a gummy solid derived from the opium poppy, is also a multi-billion-dollar revenue producer. The drug rose to prominence in Canada in the late 19th century, imported by Chinese immigrants and typically smoked. Since the late 1940s, morphine and heroin, more potent derivatives of opium, have emerged, typically injected intravenously.

What links opiates to tobacco is the user's irresistible craving for the drug. In the absence of these two drugs, physical and psychological symptoms of withdrawal typically develop. Some clinicians refer to this as drug dependence, and others would define it as drug addiction.

Clinicians usually apply the word "addiction" to continued heroin use and the word "dependence" to continued tobacco use. In large measure, this is because heroin users tend to be more socially desperate than tobacco users. A heroin habit costs about $100 per day and a tobacco habit about $7 a day — both prices artificial creations of government. The real costs of manufacturing two packs of cigarettes is about 75 cents, and the real cost of manufacturing a day's supply of opiates is similarly insignificant.

We do know that daily use of tobacco is ultimately much more damaging than daily use of opiates. If opiate use is relatively stable, the most deleterious effects are typically constipation and a somewhat reduced sex drive. These intrusions may be irritating or disappointing, but they cannot compare to the lung cancer, heart disease and emphysema that tobacco can produce.

Unlike tobacco, however, the intravenous injection of heroin can kill a user at a single sitting. This typically happens when the person injecting is misinformed or uninformed about the dose, forgetful of the a mount taken, or suicidal. A lifelong dependence on heroin can, however, be as consistent with social productivity and physical well-being as a lifelong dependence on tea or coffee.

In those societies in which smoking or eating opium is tolerated, it does not appear to be a major cause of premature death. In the industrialized world, however, an epidemic of lung cancer and heart disease has followed the mass production and promotion of the modern cigarette.

The division between legal and illegal drugs was created in Canada in 1908, but the story really begins with the second Opium War in the 1850s. Britain had gone to war in order to impose the opium traffic on China. The Chinese government fought the introduction of the drug into their country, but the Empire was ultimately successful, and by the late 19th century, opium smoking was a popular pastime in China.

When Canadian industrialists came looking for cheap labour to build the industries of western Canada, they came to China, offering labourers about 10 times the amount they could earn for comparable work at home. Thousands of Chinese moved to Vancouver annually to work on the construction of the Canadian Pacific Railway and to build other segments of the industrial infrastructure. They were paid about half what white workers received.

Between 1870 and 1908, a number of Chinese merchants operated opium factories in the B.C. cities of Vancouver, Victoria and New Westminster; each paid a municipal licensing fee. The factories, seldom the object of public concern, produced a black tar opium that was purchased equally by white and Chinese customers, and typically smoked.

The white pharmacies of the day also sold opiated tonics, elixirs and analgesics to their customers as patent medicines. The medical profession and the burgeoning patent-medicine industry were hailing opium as a panacea; cocaine and alcohol were also active ingredients in many of the industry's products.

In the late 19th century, these concoctions of opium, alcohol and cocaine were the physician's preferred remedies for emotional or psychological distress. But, by the early 20th century, this alliance of doctors and entrepreneurs began to falter. In their advertisements, the patent-medicine makers urged Americans and Canadians to medicate themselves in order to avoid the expense and unnecessary intrusion of physicians and pharmacists.

The patent-medicine industry was becoming an economic threat to physicians. Medicine was transforming itself from an art to a science, and into professional associations with both economic and social objectives. By the early 20th century, the Canadian Medical Association and the Canadian Pharmaceutical Association were becoming politically powerful organizations, opposed to what they called "the quackery" of the patent-medicine companies.

The realities of opiate dependence and cocaine abuse were gradually being recognized, just as medicine was dramatically extending human longevity. While most of this was accomplished through a fairly basic understanding of the importance of personal hygiene in the transmission of disease, there were also increasing successes in surgical intervention and, later in the century, in the development of antibiotics and other drugs.

In 1908, Canada experienced a profound shift in drug-control policy. The sale or manufacture of smoking opium was prohibited: for the first time in our history we had criminalized a psychoactive drug. Only one form of the drug was criminalized, however. Chinese smoking-opium manufacturers were to be put out of business through criminal penalties, but the patent-medicine industry could continue to dispense opiated liquids to its white customers, provided that the ingredients of the various elixirs or analgesics were set out on each bottle.

Mackenzie King was the architect of the policy of criminalization, urging this kind of legislation in the aftermath of Vancouver's anti-Asiatic riot of September 1907. A rally to support a ban on Chinese immigration had turned into a rampage into the Chinese and Japanese quarters of Vancouver. Businesses were damaged and destroyed by the angry crowd.

King, the deputy minister of labour, was sent to Vancouver to compensate the Chinese for their damages. "It should be made impossible to manufacture this drug anywhere in the Dominion," he said of smoking opium while in Vancouver, and added, "We will get some good out of this riot yet." Within two months, the federal government criminally prohibited the manufacture and sale of smoking opium.

In 1911, Mackenzie King went back to the House of Commons as the government's minister of labour. He had two requests to make of Parliament. First, King wanted to add cocaine to the schedule of prohibited drugs. He told the Commons that "the medical men" had told him cocaine was more dangerous than morphine, and he argued that use of the drug would facilitate "the seduction of our daughters and the demoralization of our young men." King had been informed by the Montreal police that cocaine was, among other things, most popular among young black men.

King also told the House of Commons that police across the country were having difficulty in obtaining convictions for sale or manufacture of opium. A new offence, "illegal drug possession," was necessary, if these battles against opium and cocaine were to succeed.

When facing questions about his new drug legislation in the House, King was asked by a member of the Conservative opposition why tobacco was not being added to the list of prohibited substances. "Tobacco has not yet been considered a drug," King, a non-smoker, shot back. He knew that tobacco was as much of a drug as opium, but was not prepared to admit publicly that opium could be taken "in much the same way that an Englishman might use a cigar, or spirits."

In 1923, marijuana was criminalized with a simple declaration in the House of Commons: "There is a new drug in the schedule." There was unanimous passage of this addition and no debate. Marijuana had been associated with Mexican migrants and black jazz musicians, and was said to be connected with madness and promiscuity.

Alcohol was also a much-discussed and debated drug during this period of history. Temperance unions were formed, spurred on, at least in part, by women who had experienced drunken beatings at the hands of husbands. In a national referendum on prohibition in 1898, a slender majority of Canadians endorsed the principle of an alcohol-free society; Wilfrid Laurier, a proponent of a "wet" Canada, declined to transform this majority view into legislation. While the temperance movement was ultimately successful in accomplishing a short-lived national prohibition in 1918, as a part of the war effort, it was never really as powerful as anti-opium, -cocaine, or -marijuana organizations. By the late 1920s, each province had repealed its prohibition legislation, and the popularity of alcohol began to climb, along with the power of the industry and the power of government to raise revenue from sales.

Possession of the drug was never criminalized, and legal initiatives generally allowed alcohol producers and distributors, even during Prohibition, to continue with both interprovincial shipments of their products and out-of-country transactions.

By the end of the roaring '20s, the way in which Canadians came to understand drug-taking had been transformed. As Toronto lawyer Mel Green has noted, what was regarded in 1900 as a matter of private indulgence was, by 1930, a matter of public evil. There were now "good" and "bad" drugs. The drugs of the blacks and the Chinese had been targeted as bad, but white European uses of alcohol and tobacco were acceptable recreations. Marijuana, opium and cocaine had been elevated to the status of a social problem, their use deserving of severe penalty.

The construction of this moral fault line was assisted by police, increasingly harsh government legislation and various propagandists. The writing of Edmonton magistrate and suffragette Emily Murphy, also known as Janey Canuck, played a critical role. Ms. Murphy's analyses of the drug problem were serialized in *Maclean's*, and printed in book form as *The Black Candle*. She feared that white women might be seduced by black men using cocaine, or by Oriental men smoking opium. Opium was described as "an attempt to injure the bright browed races of the world." "Persons using marijuana," she wrote, "smoke the dried leaves of the plant, which has the effect of driving them completely insane. The addict loses all sense of moral responsibility. Addicts to this drug, while under its influence, are immune to pain, becoming raving maniacs, and are liable to kill or indulge in any forms of violence to other persons."

But the late 1960s and early 1970s have again changed the way in which we understand drugs in our culture. From the 1920s to the 1960s, there was sporadic use of marijuana, cocaine and opium by a small and typically socially and economically marginal population: jazz musicians in the 1930s and the beatniks and the beat generation in the 1950s. But it was not until the late 1960s that illegal drug use began to cut across all social classes and political alliances. Ultimately, 100 million young Canadians and Americans made the conscious decision to commit the criminal offence of possession of marijuana. Like the Chinese opium smokers of British Columbia, marijuana users were originally economically marginal men and women who were resented and feared. Marijuana was the drug of the hippies, the young, those who questioned the values of materialist success, and those opposed to the Vietnam war.

The young were challenging the moral validity of the line between legal and illegal drugs, and the state responded by budgeting $1 million to study the problem. In Canada, the federal government appointed the Le Dain Commission, "An Inquiry into the Non-Medical Use of Drugs." The Le Dain Commission issued a final report in 1973, urging very cautious movement towards the wise exercise of freedom of choice. Specifically, it urged that possession of marijuana no longer be a criminal offence, and that heroin maintenance programs be encouraged on a closely monitored and experimental basis.

Its recommendations have been largely ignored. No government wants to be remembered as "soft on drugs" or to concede that the line between legal and illegal drugs is a rather arbitrary byproduct of our social history, rather than a matter of moral consequence.

For as long as Canada has been a nation, we have been writing moral, economic and political scripts about drugs. Amphetamines and cocaine may be pharmacologically similar, but they have different scripts attached. The image of a capitalist pharmaceutical is pitted against the image of a pagan South American powder. Taking a drug thought to be designed to restore an individual to economic productivity is, in political terms, quite a different act from taking a drug in order to obtain pleasure. When we add caffeine, alcohol, heroin, tobacco, marijuana and other pharmaceuticals to the mix, these cultural scripts and preferences only become more complex and more convoluted.

The war against drugs has very little to do with public health. It is a moral battle about the appropriate methods and reasons for alteration of consciousness, pitting the "legitimate" drugs of affluent western culture — tobacco, alcohol and pharmaceuticals — against the "bad" drugs of the developing Third World — the opium poppy, the coca plant, and cannabis and its derivatives.

The war on drugs serves various political agendas, and most pointedly those of covert military operations. The Central Intelligence Agency of the United States has been implicated in several instances; the governments of Colombia and Panama, the freedom fighters of Afghanistan and various participants in the Gulf conflict have also been said to be involved in trading guns for illegal drugs.

By condoning and occasionally participating in the traffic, these organizations accomplish a number of contradictory objectives. They reap millions of dollars from the distribution of illegal drugs, they circumvent government-imposed financial limitations on strategies of political intervention, and they, perhaps inadvertently, line the coffers of international arms dealers. When I asked Rod Stamler, head of the RCMP's drug branch from 1980 to 1989, about the role of the CIA in the business of illegal drugs, he responded, "Well, they're involved in politics, and organized criminals are involved in politics, and drugs are profit, and profits are needed to sometimes tip the balance here and there in various parts of the world."

In Canada, the war on drugs has not been closely tied to foreign policy, but it has been conscripted for political purposes, with limited success. In 1986, Prime Minister Brian Mulroney announced that there was a drug epidemic in Canada, and was promptly contradicted in the national press. There was no evidence to suggest that there had actually been increases in the use of most illegal drugs and the prime minister hadn't mentioned alcohol and tobacco.

Substance abuse, whether legal or illegal, is most fairly cast as an issue of public health, not a moral question. Ultimately, drugs are symbols of a potentially unhealthy lifestyle, and drug use is one more variable to throw into the hopper of what some people call "wellness." Drug use is relevant to health in the way that regular exercise, good nutrition and stress management are relevant to health.

The drugs that are actually killing us are the legal ones, which are rarely described as drugs. Those who operate these distribution schemes for legal drugs are typically described as captains of commerce rather than drug dealers. There is an Orwellian cant to our rhetoric. We worry about the demonic pushers of marijuana, cocaine and heroin, while we sit comfortably viewing sophisticated and costly advertisements that link beer consumption with a glamorous and exciting lifestyle. And we leaf through magazine images that link tobacco consumption to healthy and attractive men and women in pristine wilderness settings. In reality, it is the legal drugs that are pushed upon the consumer.

The intention of users — to alter ordinary waking consciousness — does not change as we move from legal to illegal drugs. In every instance, we ingest a chemical and experience a change in our minds, our bodies, or both. What counts in taking drugs is the substance, the dose taken, the mental and emotional attitude of the user, and the social setting in which consumption takes place. Less refined (and, hence, less potent) drugs are better for public health than more potent and refined drugs; smoking or injecting a drug has been shown to greatly increase the risk of dependence.

When we criminalize a particular substance, we pay attention to only a small part of this picture. Criminalization is a metaphor for war, a battle in which the domestic military are asked to arrest and convict those who possess certain psychoactives. And this war on drugs, like all other wars, is a statement of human failure. There aren't so much good or bad drugs as there are good and bad relationships with drugs.

Some drugs are more dangerous than others, however, both in terms of their effects and in terms of the way in which they have been integrated into our culture.

What we are doing now isn't working. High rates of premature death are more closely tied to legal drugs than they are to illegal drugs, even when differences in rates of use are taken into account. Moreover, death is less likely from illegal-drug use than from illegal-drug distribution and its control. We are at war with ourselves, and if we can better understand the dimensions of these battles, we might be able to find a more peaceful resolution of our conflict.

IAIN BENSON

The Benson home on Bowen Island is one-part nursery, two parts cultural centre. Given their burgeoning family — Iain and Eleanor now have five children — no one was surprised in 1990 when the renovations began on the tiny cottage they had been living in for the previous three years. But the community was delighted to find that much of the new structure was given over to a library and music room in which the Bensons now frequently hold recitals and lectures. A CD of a classical concert by the Shih Sisters, recorded there this year, is due for release about the same time as this book.

Iain is a lawyer, practising constitutional and administrative law and acting as the Senior Research Fellow for the Centre for Renewal in Public Policy, Ottawa. He is also editing Vol. 7 of *The Collected Works of G.K. Chesterton* for Ignatius Books of San Francisco and New York.

He would like to thank Eleanor Benson and Dr. Ted Spear for their helpful comments and suggestions on his contribution here. He also would like to thank Professor Loren Wilkinson for providing the forum within which many of these ideas were first developed.

Goodness, Values and Community: Compasses with Damaged Needles

How often do we hear people speaking of "values"? The term appears everywhere in all sorts of settings, especially those with an ethical or social dimension. You would think that those values must be important and well-understood to occupy such a key role in discussions. But do we know what we mean when we speak of "our values"? When we speak of "my values" in relation to "your values" or "social values" or "community values," do we know what we mean? We know that there is a search for meaning in the broader sense; this is clear from a review of the latest books on the store shelves. But does our quest for meaning encompass the application of this key term "values"? This essay will explore the term; its history, its use and its relation to the term "goodness" before attempting to draw a conclusion about the term "values".

Judging by the bookstore shelves, today's society seems fascinated with "healing" and "self-help." In philosophy, too, many writers speak of a need to restore wholeness or to deepen "authenticity" as a means of overcoming society's problems. Many books about the nature of the individual in North American society speak of alienation, atomism, loneliness, narcissism and individualism. This essay will also attempt to link this longing for wholeness and meaning with an aspect of current language that points to a loss of learning which severely inhibits our ability to speak of goodness with conviction.

The rise of insecurity about what is "good" and "bad" affects all aspects of society. Because the law must deal with fundamental notions of right and wrong, court judgments can provide some of the best examples of how clearly we think (or do not think) about truth. The courts determine what the law is and how it applies to specific disputes. That function has always been important in affirming the symbolic role of law as well as its practical outworkings. People will never stop murdering one another, but it is important to maintain our collective revulsion for murder by keeping the law against it on the books, the penalties severe and the enforcement as effective as possible.

Legal judgments do not deal with these broader philosophical questions in any comprehensive way. However, where the courts are discussing "fundamental rights and freedoms," as they must be in evaluating the *Charter of Rights and Freedoms* that Canada adopted in 1982, judges must occasionally venture out upon deeper philosophical waters. Even in doing so, the courts are wary about discussing the nature of human flourishing and human happiness. This is understandable given the status of legal (and general) education, which for many years has not dealt seriously with philosophical concepts. In fact, a rigorous examination of philosophy is not required in most Canadian law schools; courses in the technique of law, not the purpose of law, dominate. This separation of technique from purpose is visible in every area of human endeavour and reflects the separation of articulated philosophy from education.

It was Aristotle who noted that an effect is proportionate to its cause. Such a wide-spread separation of technique from purpose must have a wide-spread cause. Many have suggested that education is that cause; or, rather, the failure of education. Some have said that education — which would require a grounding in these deeper areas — has been replaced by "schooling." This has forsaken the traditional idea of education, in which the liberal arts were the *artes liberales,* from the latin root for freedom: learning about the truth, which is eternal, freed us from the chains of our particular time.

Whether the problem is education or not, the separation of technique from purpose has contributed, perhaps indirectly, to our inability to confront the issue of goodness. Until we acknowledge this inability, this hesitance, it will be difficult to move in any better direction. "Better," after all, is itself an evaluative concept that involves judgment against a standard. A thing can be said to be better only if there is a standard against which it can be measured. The basis of all philosophy is the belief that there are better and worse things. The challenge is in identifying the basis on which we say some things are better or worse than others.

In his book, *Ten Philosophical Mistakes,* Mortimer J. Adler offers this first principle of all moral philosophy: "We ought to desire whatever is really good for us and nothing else."[1] In Chapter 5, *Moral Values,* Adler points out the history of the mistakes that end up reducing moral judgments to mere opinion. He notes that unless there is a similarity of human needs for all human beings everywhere "… we would have no basis for a global doctrine that calls for the protection of human rights by all the nations of the earth" (p.127).

I suspect that few would endorse this statement today: they have been taught that "goods," like "values," are relative, one person's not being the same as the others. Yet, I do not believe that we occupy a world of such confident and strident relativism. Rather, our discussion has become obscured by language which, in its ambiguity, masks the fact that we share many common values because we believe them to be "good" and hope that others do, too. In holding such views, moreover, we assert that such concepts are "good" not because we think they are but because they are, in the nature of things — in reality— good.

To take an extravagant example: few would agree with people who said that, by their "value system," they believed it was a good thing to rob banks at gunpoint. We recognize that "values" can differ but we do not allow "values" to act as a cover for actions that we consider corrupt.

Let us look closer at the term "values." When we speak of our values, we seldom consider them to be purely individual. We expect that others have an obligation to respect our values, not just because they are ours but because we consider them worthy of respect or, say, good for society. While we may take it as a foundational principle that "my values" and "your values" are necessarily personal, we still mean them or hope them to be shared.

At a conference on medical ethics that I recently attended, speaker after speaker referred to such concepts as "community values," "shared values" and "fundamental values." These speakers apparently thought the concepts had some validity beyond personal commitment. How is a "fundamental value" fundamental if it can be accepted or rejected by any particular person? Recall Mortimer Adler's point about "human rights" having meaning because we recognize a broad validity to such rights. We would be unlikely to accept the position of a national leader who said: "Those human rights are your values, they are not the values of my country." We would counter by saying that such "values" ought to be recognized by all countries. But once we insert the term "ought," we have stepped beyond a personal or culturally based use of the language of "values" — or, at the very least, highlighted a problem of using such an ambiguous language.

The term "values" — as we understand it today — is itself very recent. It came into Western usage from Nietzsche, the German philosopher of will. Nietzsche advocated the triumph and domination of the will. He spoke of the need to have a "transvaluation of all values" in which goodness would be only what we willed it to be and not what was given to us in the nature of things. Wills were constantly in a power struggle and the most powerful would (and should) triumph.

The person generally considered to have been Canada's leading political philosopher, the late George Grant, was one of the clearest writers on the phenomenon of "values language" which, as he once noted in a Canadian Broadcasting Corporation interview is "... an obscuring language for morality, once the idea of purpose has been destroyed. And that's why it is so widespread in North America."[2]

Although Grant's writings are not yet as well known in Canada as they should be, he is acknowledged as the philosopher who has best expressed the problematic nature of the term "values" in modern discourse. In a preface to the American publication of Grant's book, *English-speaking Justice*, Stanley Hauerwas and Alasdair MacIntyre wrote:

> Grant's writings on moral and political theory ... are among the most interesting North American work in that area to be produced since 1945; and they are almost entirely unknown in the United States ... Grant exhibits, as few recent writers on moral and political theory do, a consistent attempt to speak immediately to the peculiar needs of time and place ... [in his writings since 1965] Grant has drawn upon Nietzsche and Heidegger to develop a systematic critique of modernity, one that makes it urgent to identify what resources from the past are left to us which will enable us to preserve traditions of justice and civility in dark times....[3]

Grant himself wrote:

> Everybody uses the word 'values' to describe our making of the world ... capitalists and socialists, atheists and avowed believers, scientists and politicians. The word comes to us so platitudinously that we take it to belong to the way things are. It is forgotten that before Nietzsche and his immediate predecessors, men did not think about their actions in that language. They did not think they made the world valuable, but that they participated in its goodness.[4]

The term "values" is often used in areas of moral debate to bridge the gap between a purely personal language of meaning and a sense that there must be shared goods. The need for a bridge is obvious, but these language bridges can obscure rather than facilitate meaningful dialogue about goodness. This is an important point because language is central to our defence of goodness itself. Corrupt a people's ability to speak about goodness and truth and you soon hamper their ability to think about goodness and truth. Language is related to thought and thought precedes action. Garbled language about truth eventually disables the ability to act and virtuous action is seen in classical philosophy to be a key to human happiness itself. The Biblical account of the Tower of Babel and Orwell's accounts of language manipulation in his novel *Nineteen Eighty-Four* both speak to the relationship between language, meaning and human purposes. This begins to explain why books on self-help and healing are so prevalent at the very time when our language about virtue and goodness has become so confused. How ironic that our search for meaning is undercut by a language which, in its relativistic ambiguity, precludes the meaning we seek in its use: our compasses have damaged needles.

What has occurred, in part, is that the belief in intrinsic worth (which is the *Oxford English Dictionary* definition of the word "value") has been replaced with the idea that the individual him or herself determines (or creates) worth, there being nothing "out there" to discover. Such usage of the term "value" may have plausibility when one is discussing aesthetic choices such as cut of clothes. Such use, however, becomes erroneous when, for example, "the value of human life" is being discussed. Yet the modern use does not make a distinction and renders all "value" ultimately personal.

In Canada, one frequently hears that it is improper for people to attempt to force their personal values on others by way of law. This presupposes that there is such a thing as a "value-free" law, whereas law is about norms, and normative statements, no matter how one may attempt to dress them up, are not value-neutral. But note how far from any sense of "intrinsic" worth such a notion of "value" has come. There is no basis upon which to assume that what consensus achieves will bear any relationship to an objective truth.

"Consensus" is another word that can rightly join the list of those which, if not properly understood, merely obscures attempts to address moral truth. In fact, we have lost sight of the very notion of objective truth. The ubiquitous use of "values" language demonstrates the extent to which the moral universe many of us think we inhabit has been ignored (or usurped) by modern relativistic notions which, if we recognized them, we would reject.

We can see examples of value relativism everywhere. It is particularly prevalent in debates relating to ethics. Sue Rodriguez, who so narrowly failed to get the Supreme Court of Canada to find a constitutional right to physician-assisted suicide, expressed the modern view succinctly: "Why on earth would anyone want to impose their own value system on me? I've got mine, they've got theirs."[5]

The euthanasia debate that is raging in Canada and in several other countries provides an interesting example of the indeterminacy of "values" language. Professor Eike-Henner W. Kluge, an expert in medical ethics in Canada, in a recent presentation before the Senate Special Committee on Euthanasia and Assisted Suicide, gave an example of modern "values" usage when he said:

> Everyone is embedded in a social context, and that context shapes our expectations but also our values. There are two points that are important here, namely: that values are the primary determinate of how individuals will exercise a particular right, and second, that members of society usually come to accept the values of the society in which they are embedded. ... Consequently, if a proxy decision-maker has been given no values to use, the proxy cannot make a decision, in which case the proxy decision-maker is faced with the obligation of making a decision but not having the tools with which to make it.
>
> Proxy decision-makers, therefore, have two options. They may use their own values, or they may use the values of the social context in which the incompetent person is embedded. ... The first is ethically unacceptable. The second is correct. It is the only way in which it is possible to exercise the right of choice for the now incompetent individual.
>
> Therefore, I submit that people whose values differ from the societal context have an obligation to inform others that this is the case, lest for want of such notice they should be treated according to prevailing societal values and receive treatment which their values would label anathema. Correlatively, society has the right to assume that people who have not given indication of such difference share the prevailing societal values.
>
> This brings me to the exception. If previously competent persons have made no disposition, if a decision must be made, and if, finally, the prevailing societal values would be in favour of deliberate death under the circumstances, then the duly empowered proxy decision-maker must request deliberate death. In fact, for the proxy not to act in this fashion or for society to refuse to honour such a proxy request would be for society to discriminate against the incompetent person on the basis of handicap.[6]

If we accept, however, that values are merely personal, the product of autonomous will, where do we go to find "societal values"? How do we know that "societal values" bear any relation to what is "good"? History, even contemporary history, is full of situations in which societies do things most would consider wrong or unjust. Do we actually believe that results of polls, or the desires of the majority are satisfactory ways of determining over time what is "right" and "wrong" in society?

The Royal Commission on New Reproductive Technologies, in its recent report, said it thought not and for this reason decided to disregard the views of the majority of Canadians, who did not believe that lesbians should have access to donor insemination:

> The Commission believes that society's approach to new reproductive technologies should be governed by the social values of Canadians. We

are also aware, however, of the difference between social values and individual opinions. We believe that social values held by Canadians are reflected in the *Canadian Charter of Rights and Freedoms,* and the prohibitions on discrimination it contains must be our guide in this matter.[7]

In *The Poison of Subjectivism,* C.S. Lewis comments on the different way in which moderns view "judgments of value." He states:

> Until modern times, no thinker of the first rank ever doubted that our judgments of value were rational judgments or that what they discovered was objective. ... The modern view is very different. It does not believe that value judgments are really judgments at all. They are sentiments, or complexes, or attitudes, produced in a community by the pressure of its environment and its traditions, and differing from one community to another. To say that a thing is good is merely to express our feeling about it, and our feeling about it is the feeling we have been socially conditioned to have.[8]

This "modern view," of which Lewis and Grant and many others are so critical, is strikingly like that expressed by Professor Kluge. Lewis soundly rejected what he termed "the fatal superstition that men can create values, that a community can choose its 'ideology' as men choose their clothes."

Lewis objects that:

> This whole attempt to jettison traditional values as something subjective and to substitute a new scheme of values for them is wrong. It is like trying to lift yourself by your own coat collar. Let us get two propositions written into our minds with indelible ink: 1) The human mind has no more power of inventing a new value than of planting a new sun in the sky or a new primary colour in the spectrum; 2) Every attempt to do so consists in arbitrarily selecting some one maxim of traditional morality, isolating it from the rest, and erecting it into an *unum necessarium.*[9]

> This impossibility of creating values means that one must take certain things as one finds them: Either the maxims of traditional morality must be accepted as axioms of practical reason which neither admit nor require argument to support them and not to 'see' which is to have lost human status; or else there are no values at all, what we mistook for values being 'projections' of irrational emotions.[10]

As Lewis says by way of summation, "... a philosophy which does not accept value as eternal and objective can lead us only to ruin"[11] and:

> If 'good' means only the local ideology, how can those who invent the local ideology be guided by any idea of good themselves? The very idea of freedom presupposes some objective moral law which overarches rulers

and ruled alike. Subjectivism about values is eternally incompatible with democracy. We and our rulers are of one kind only so long as we are subject to one law. But if there is no Law of Nature, the ethos of any society is the creation of its rulers, educators and conditioners; and every creator stands above and outside his own creation. Unless we return to the crude and nursery-like belief in objective values, we perish.[12]

The essay *The Poison of Subjectivism*, appeared in 1943, the same year as *The Abolition of Man*, in which Lewis referred to "... the half-hearted skeptics who still hope to find 'real' values when they have debunked the traditional ones. This is the rejection of the concept of value altogether."[13]

Again Lewis asserts that "a dogmatic belief in objective value is necessary to the very idea of a rule which is not tyranny or an obedience which is not slavery."[14]

In this book more than any other he wrote, Lewis succinctly sets out the cardinal difference between the approach of the ancients and the moderns by stating that:

> For the wise men of old, the cardinal problem had been how to conform the soul to reality, and the solution had been knowledge, self-discipline and virtue. For magic and applied science alike, the problem is how to subdue reality to the wishes of men: the solution is a technique; and both, in the practice of this technique, are ready to do things hitherto regarded as disgusting and impious ... .[15]

Throughout the centuries many of the greatest thinkers have discussed the importance of learning and of preserving the central truths which define the society. These truths are not relative or subjective but transcendent. Scientist and social scientist Michael Polanyi has written that:

> ... the adherents of a great tradition are largely unaware of their own premises, which lie deeply embedded in the unconscious foundations of practice ... if the citizens are dedicated to certain transcendent obligations and particularly to such general ideals as truth, justice, charity, and these are embodied in the tradition of the community to which allegiance is maintained, a great many issues between citizens, and all to some extent, can be left — and are necessarily left — for the individual consciences to decide. The moment, however, a community ceases to be dedicated through its members to transcendent ideals, it can continue to exist undisrupted only by submission to a single centre of unlimited secular power.[16]

That many people in our society "are largely unaware of their own [moral and ethical] premises" is a fact. The foregoing is a body of opinion that ought not to be ignored, a body of opinion that states categorically both that it is necessary to know transcendent ideals (such as the "sanctity of human life" or "the inherent dignity of the human person" or "the essential wrongness of actively taking innocent life") and also that the modern age is rife with a language that obscures purpose and leads to a rampant and lonely individualism. As was said in the influential book *Habits of the Heart:*

> We have never before faced a situation that called our deepest assumptions so radically into question. Our problems today are not just political. They are moral and have to do with the meaning of life. We have assumed that as long as economic growth continued, we could leave all else to the private sphere. Now that economic growth is faltering and moral ecology on which we have tacitly depended is in disarray, we are beginning to understand that our common life requires more than an exclusive concern for material consumption.[17]

Certain contemporary writers have written about the effect of failing to teach the precepts of traditional morality and the difficulty that modern ethical theories pose to our understanding of ourselves in the modern age. These writers are invaluable for understanding what has happened and is happening to us on the moral level.[18]

In various ways, they comment on different aspects of the emotivism that now passes for moral discussion. "Emotivism," which dovetails with "values language," is defined by Alasdair MacIntyre in *After Virtue,* as:

> The doctrine that all evaluative judgments and more specifically all moral judgments are nothing but expressions of preference, expressions of attitude or feeling, insofar as they are moral or evaluative in character ... moral judgments, being expressions of attitude or feeling, are neither true nor false; and agreement in moral judgment is not to be secured by any rational method, for there are none. It is to be secured, if at all, by producing certain non-rational effects on the emotions or attitudes of those who disagree with one. We use moral judgments not only to express our own feelings and attitudes, but also precisely to produce such effects in others.[19]

Such a development, MacIntyre continues, has led to a situation in which "... morality has to some large degree disappeared — and this marks a degeneration, a grave cultural loss."[20]

These writers point out that such a diminution of the moral framework in theory has not, in all circumstances, been represented in practice. They note, for example, how many people will accept uncritically the notion that "values" are merely personal, and then will make comments indicating that they subscribe to concepts of objective good. Thus, people may, in one breath, enunciate a view that morals are purely subjective and, in the next, condemn apartheid, environmental polluters or Colombian drug barons — and yet remain oblivious to the contradiction. We are becoming incapable of speaking within a normal social context about things which we consider must still be objectively true.[21]

The situation as far as judges are concerned is more dire because of the practical consequences of their philosophical impoverishment. They are vested with the duty to interpret the *Canadian Charter of Rights and Freedoms:* in doing so they are forced, in this vacuum of education, to give meaning to such general (and deeply philosophical) concepts as "freedom of association," "freedom of religion," "security of the person," etc. At a conference a few years ago at the University of British Columbia, the recently retired Supreme Court of Canada Justice, Mr. Willard Estey, who should be admired for his candour, stated that the judges are not trained in the very area for which we are looking to them for guidance.

These difficulties have their counterparts in all disciplines. It is after all, a matter of great debate whether the current forms of "liberal" philosophies can provide a sufficient basis for moral or ethical analysis in society. We should be wary of trying to make all liberal philosophies fit the same category (for there are many differences between them).

George Grant, however, offers a useful definition of liberalism, which makes a link between these current philosophies and the individual will. It is the issue of the due limits of individual will, after all, that is at the centre of so many issues in Canadian society, such as the current euthanasia debate. Grant's definition is:

> A set of beliefs which proceed from the central assumption that man's essence is his freedom and therefore that what chiefly concerns man in this life is to shape the world as we want it.[22]

In a critique of one of the most influential American juridical theorists, John Rawls, Grant observed:

> When contractual liberals hold within their thought remnants of secularized Christianity or Judaism, these remnants, if made conscious, must be known as unthinkable in terms of what is given in the modern. How, in modern thought, can we find positive answers to the questions: i) what is it about human beings that makes liberty and equality their due? (ii) why is justice what we are fitted for, when it is not convenient? Why is it our good? The inability of contractual liberals (or indeed Marxists) to answer these questions is the terrifying darkness which has fallen upon modern justice.[23]

The meaning of justice has generally vanished from legal studies; few Canadian law schools require courses in the history of legal philosophy. In a stinging indictment of modern education and its effect on the system of justice, George Grant said this of the Canadian judiciary:

> The living forth of the triumph of the will among the strongest advocates of complete liberty for abortion does not imply that such advocates are in any sense a core for fascist politics. They simply give us a taste now of what politics will be like when influential groups in society think meaning is found in getting what they want most deeply at all costs. They illustrate what pressure this puts upon a legal system rooted in liberalism, whose leaders have not been educated in what that rootedness comprises. Even in its highest ranks the legal system in its unthinking liberalism simply flounders in the face of those who find meaning in the triumph of the will. This has been shown in both of the liberally appointed American and Canadian judiciaries. When society puts power into the hands of the courts, they had better be educated ... The more the justices quote philosophy or religious tradition the less they give the sense they understand what they are dealing with.[24]

There are many examples of the difficulty the courts are having in articulating a coherent approach to fundamental issues in society. The *Rodriguez* case itself was such an example. I would like to examine another case, one in which the nine judges of the court were unanimous,[25] but, as shown below, incoherent.

The case of *R. v. Butler* [1992] 2 W.W.R. 577 involved the definition of obscenity in the *Criminal Code*. In upholding the definition against a Charter challenge on the basis of the "freedom of expression," the court was at pains to attempt to base the restriction on pornography on the "harm" it does, even though the court could not establish a clear causal connection between the existence of pornography and harm arising from it. While the court could not avoid the fact that such a restriction depends upon a moral basis, it undercut the ability to determine a valid ground for moral evaluation by saying that such valuation must be found in the Charter itself.

This is nonsensical because the Charter is an open-ended document that states its rights in outline and in the broadest of terms. The court, in dealing with a Charter case, once it has found a breach of a guaranteed right, must determine whether the breach or limitation is justified in a free and democratic society; and this is an external analysis, involving matters not to be found in the Charter. The court, by seeking to avoid a particular moral framework, cannot erect any moral framework and instead creates a circular approach that makes moral articulation impossible.

Mr. Justice Sopinka stated, at pp. 606-607, that it is no longer an appropriate objective of law "… to advance a particular conception of morality" and that:

> … this particular objective is no longer defensible in view of the Charter. To impose a certain standard of public and sexual morality, solely because it reflects the conventions of a given community, is inimical to the exercise and enjoyment of individual freedoms, which form the basis of our social contract. D. Dyzenhaus, *Obscenity and the Charter: Autonomy and Equality* (1991), 1 C.R. (4th) 367 at p. 270, refers to this as 'legal moralism,' of a majority deciding what values should inform individual lives and then coercively imposing those values on minorities. The prevention of 'dirt for dirt's sake' is not a legitimate objective which would justify the violation of one of the most fundamental freedoms enshrined in the Charter.
>
> On the other hand, I cannot agree with the suggestion of the appellant that Parliament does not have the right to legislate on the basis of some fundamental conception of morality for the purposes of safeguarding the values which are integral to a free and democratic society. As Dyzenhaus writes (at p. 376), 'Moral disapprobation is recognized as an appropriate response when it has its basis in Charter values.'
>
> … much of the criminal law is based on moral conceptions of right and wrong and the mere fact that a law is grounded in morality does not automatically render it illegitimate.

Justice Sopinka then recognized that moral corruption and harm to society are inextricably linked and "it is moral corruption of a certain kind which leads to the detrimental effect on society" (p. 608). But if that is the case, and Parliament has the right to legislate "on the basis of some fundamental conception of morality" then it is not possible to avoid "a particular conception of morality." Even at its most basic level, if Parliament legislates, it would necessarily adopt a particular conception of morality. Yet this was the very thing that Justice Sopinka said at the outset was "no longer appropriate."

This is just another example of the epistemological insecurity (or incoherence) of modern justice. The process of justice must deal with matters that raise moral issues and competing philosophical approaches that could tax (and have taxed) the most learned of philosophers. With this sort of analysis from Canada's highest court, one wonders how much longer Canadian society can afford to continue forms of schooling (at all levels) that avoid an articulation of philosophy and a concomitant analysis of purposes as well as techniques.

In conclusion, our contemporary expression of longings for things that are good provides a hope that we are not, in fact, relativists. We believe that it is good to care for the weak and to provide comfort to the lonely and justice for the oppressed. The corollary must be that we recognize that it is wrong to ignore those who suffer or to permit continued injustice. In short, there are "rights" and "wrongs" whether or not people acknowledge them. The fact that we speak of "rights" and "wrongs" in a language of "values" that is at best ambiguous is a clue to a deeper moral and educational impoverishment. It is true that "the heart has its reasons which reason cannot comprehend" but it is also true that reason can offer a justification for action that can convince and inform those who feel that we ought to do good but do not know how to argue that we should.

Is it not a part of a full life to talk and to debate about the nature of life and love and goodness? In so doing we are in a world that is much richer than this dominant world of ambiguous "values." This new world, in its implicit but uneasy relativism, cuts us off from the truths we may or may not share but which it is essential that we discuss. Even in our disagreements we share more than we do when speaking to ourselves in the mirror of our "personal values."

In discussing the approach that Socrates took to knowledge, Sir R.W. Livingstone wrote at p. xix of his *Portrait of Socrates* (Oxford: Clarendon, 1938):

> The true approach to knowledge was not through books or lectures, but through conversation, discussion, question and answer, two or more persons beating a subject up and down, till the chaff is winnowed from the wheat . ...

If we care about goodness and the community that is an aspect of goodness, we must challenge the meaninglessness of "values". Until we do, we shall not be able to speak meaningfully (or with authenticity) about goodness and community, how to pursue them, or what they mean for us as persons who are intimately bound to one another by the nature of our lives. It is an understanding of this "binding" that is so desperately needed in order that we can be truly free.

FOOTNOTES

1. Mortimer J. Adler, *Ten Philosophical Mistakes* (Macmillan: New York, 1985) p. 125.
2. *The Moving Image of Eternity*, written and produced by David Cayley, CBC *Ideas*, January 27, February 3, 10, 1986 (rebroadcast since then) transcript p. 17.
3. *English-speaking Justice* (Notre Dame: Notre Dame U.P.,1985) p.p. vi-vii
4. *Time as History* (Toronto: CBC,1969) p.p. 44-45.
5. Quoted in Lisa Hobbs Birnie, *Uncommon Will: The Death and Life of Sue Rodriguez* (Toronto: Macmillan, 1994) p. 116.
6. Eike-Henner W. Kluge, Proceedings of the Senate Special Committee on Euthanasia and Assisted Suicide, (Thursday, March 17, 1994) Issue No. 2, at p.p. 20-21.
7. *Proceed With Care, Report of The Royal Commission on New Reproductive Technologies* (Ottawa: Canadian Communications Group, 1993) at p. 456.
8. *The Poison of Subjectivism*, in Walter Hooper ed., *Christian Reflections* (London: Bles, 1967) p.p. 72 -81 at 73.
9. ibid. p. 75.
10. ibid. p.p. 74 - 75.
11. ibid. p. 75.
12. ibid. p. 81.
13. *The Abolition of Man* (New York: Macmillan, 1947) at p. 33.
14. ibid. p. 46.
15. ibid. p. 48.
16. *Science, Faith and Society* (Chicago: Chicago Univ. Press, 1966) p. 76.
17. Robert N. Bellah et al. *Habits of the Heart* (New York: Harper & Row, 1986) p. 295.
18. In addition to the books listed in these footnotes, see: Mortimer J. Adler, *Reforming Education* (New York: Macmillan, 1988); Allan Bloom, *The Closing of the American Mind* (New York: Simon and Schuster, 1987); Robert George, *Making Men Moral: Civil Liberties and Public Morality* (Oxford: Clarendon, 1993); Christopher Lasch, *The Culture of Narcissism* (New York: Warner, 1979); Alasdair MacIntyre's, *Whose Justice? Which Rationality?* (Notre Dame: University of Notre Dame, 1988).
19. Alasdair MacIntyre, *After Virtue* (Notre Dame: University of Notre Dame, 2nd ed., 1984) p.p. 11-12.
20. ibid. p. 22.
21. Yet, in being critical of subjectivism, Charles Taylor makes an important point in *Sources of the Self* (Cambridge: Harvard University Press, 1989) at p. 511:

> We have to avoid the error of declaring those goods invalid whose exclusive pursuit leads to contemptible or disastrous consequences. The search for pure subjective expressive fulfilment may make life thin and insubstantial, may ultimately undercut itself. ... but that by itself does

nothing to show that subjective fulfilment is not a good. It shows only that it needs to be part of a 'package,' to be sought within a life which is also aimed at other goods ... a dilemma doesn't invalidate the riv al goods. On the contrary, it presupposes them.

And see, also, Taylor's brief and helpful *The Malaise of Modernity*, (Toronto: Anansi, 1991), where this theme is further developed.

22. *Technology and Empire* (Toronto: Anansi, 1969) at p. 114.

23. *English-speaking Justice* (Toronto: Anansi, 1985) at p. 86. Charles Taylor, in *Sources of the Self*, at p.89, comments that Rawls' central contention, that we develop a notion of justice starting only with a "thin theory of the good," is "... on the deepest level incoherent."

24. George Grant *The Triumph of the Will*, in Ian Gentles, ed. *A Time to Choose Life* (Toronto: Stoddart, 1990) p.p. 9-18 at p. 18

25. In giving the majority judgment, Mr. Justice John Sopinka spoke for himself and six other judges. The minority reasons of Gonthier J. agreed with those parts of Sopinka's judgment here referred to. On the analysis being discussed, therefore, the nine judges of the Supreme Court of Canada were unanimous.

PETER CLARKE

Among the houses of literary excellence on Bowen Island, none can match "Foxbarn" — the home of Peter Clarke and Maria Tippett — for output and high academic standard. Both teach at Cambridge University in England for part of the year and then repair to the peace and solitude of Bowen to write.

Maria Tippett, whose offering appears on Page 81, is the homegrown talent: she was born and bred in B.C. and has kept a house on Bowen since 1983. She was, therefore, high on the list when it came to looking for contributors for this book. After indicating an interest herself, she added, "Perhaps you might like my husband to write something for you."

Your husband writes?

"Oh, yes," she said. "Although he's quite busy now. He's working on *The History of Britain* for Penguin Books."

In later conversations, Peter Clarke seemed embarrassed by this reference. "Oh, no," he said. "Penguin is producing a 10-volume history. I'm only doing the 20th century."

Only, indeed.

Here then is one of Britain's foremost authorities on the 20th century with a critique of one of the century's foremost authoritarians. This review of Margaret Thatcher's book originally appeared in *The Cambridge Review.*

Thatcherism: The Downing Street Years

It is not every literary novice, blushing diffidently over her first manuscript, who easily finds a publisher, still less one prepared to pay an advance of several million pounds. But not every first author has such a story to tell. Margaret Thatcher already has an unbeatable record as Britain's longest-serving prime minister of the 20th century. It was the previous record holder, Herbert Henry Asquith (1908-16), who first established the notion that retired prime ministers write their memoirs, and he did so under a twin motivation which was not peculiar to himself. He sought vindication and he was after the money.

Asquith had acquired a reputation as a man of letters — literally so. His correspondence with a series of personable women half his age was both a relaxation while he was in office and a source of vivid "contemporary notes" when it came to padding out the otherwise ponderous tomes produced in his retirement. If Asquith affected to be the last of the amateurs, the man who displaced him from the premiership, David Lloyd George (1916-1922), showed how to professionalize the whole business. His were war memoirs in more than one sense: refighting a war of attrition over thousands of pages and drawing upon a vast arsenal of documents, selectively marshalled by an obedient staff.

In this, as in other ways, he was both setting an example to Winston Churchill (1940-45, 1951-55) and learning from him. For it was said of Churchill's own thick volumes on the First World War that he had in fact written his autobiography under the title *The World Crisis.* Similarly, his six volumes, *The Second World War,* made out his own case and cashed in on his international reputation while it was at its peak. Churchill's quip that he was confident of the verdict of history since he intended to write that history himself was more than a joke. His effrontery in walking off with all his official papers, as his personal war souvenirs, gave him an immense advantage in the battle of the books. The big mistake Neville Chamberlain (1937-40) made was to die prematurely, leaving no final testament to posterity, and Stanley Baldwin (1923, 1924-29, 1935-37), too, misspending his 10 years in retirement, remained politically intestate. Little wonder that their posthumous reputations plummeted while a whole new generation was brought up on Churchill's version of events.

There is a terrible lesson to be learned here, and most post-war prime ministers have learned it. Clement Attlee (1945-51), to be sure, produced only a slim volume of memoirs which was frankly inconsequential. It was not called *As It Happened,* in prospect of any definitive German translation under the title *Wie es eigentlich gewesen war.* But Attlee remedied the situation in other ways, notably through interviews, which put his longevity to good use and saw his stock appreciate. Anthony Eden (1955-56) and Harold Macmillan (1957-63) both followed Churchill's example with multi-volume sets of memoirs, employing assiduous research assistants to build the documentary ramparts. Harold Wilson (1964-70, 1974-76) might well have done the same, to judge from his interim account of his first government, but was subsequently disabled from defending his own record — which suffered as a result. Sir Alec Douglas Home (1963-64) was perfunctory; James Callaghan (1976-79) turned in a book, written by rote, which was neither graceful nor disgraceful; and poor Edward Heath (1970-74) proved unable or unwilling to perform at all.

The model for the Thatcher memoirs is clearly the blockbuster tradition which reached its apogee with Churchill. She has, of course, been helped in their production, as she acknowledges, by Robin Harris, acting as her "sherpa" in retrieving the official papers to which an ex-prime minister has privileged access. This grounds her account on documentary foundations, sometimes quoted or cited directly, which ensures that it cannot simply be brushed aside. Sometimes, to be sure, solidity gives way to stolidity. There is more than one whole chapter here which reads as a dutiful recapitulation of contemporary minutes, briefing papers, letters, dossiers, speeches, press releases and other material exhumed from forgotten files and now reinterred for posterity. Thatcher herself comments on officials papers that "their very dryness confirmed in my mind the value of writing this book. Some stories you have to live in order to tell."

Her claim is borne out by her text. In the midst of the most arid chronicle, when the reader's spirits have been lowered by a numbing enumeration of deadening detail, relentlessly retailed, there comes a thrilling shift of gear as we encounter an altogether different tone. Ah, we sigh, the voice of the lady herself!

But how can we know? The role of John O'Sullivan as ghostwriter is also acknowledged in the preface and there is a fine game to be played in speculating on his influence from internal evidence. For example, take the account of Thatcher's encounter with Tunku Abdul Rahman as host of the Commonwealth summit in Malaysia in 1989. Thatcher records how surprisingly displeased he seemed when she told him that it had been a mistake to exclude South Africa from the Commonwealth: "I soon learned why. He told me that he had been principally responsible for throwing South Africa out in the first place. Clang." Here is an endearingly human touch in an otherwise bland account — and we must trust that it was Thatcher who applied it.

What register can we recognize as her own voice? And what range of allusion gives an authentic insight into her own mental universe? There is an arresting passage which focuses on Jim Prior as just the sort of Tory "wet" whom Thatcher despised: "I call such figures 'the false squire'. They have the outward show of a John Bull — ruddy face, white hair, bluff manner — but inwardly they are political calculators who see the task of Conservatives as one of retreating gracefully before the Left's inevitable advance." This is a fine image, and surely a revealing one.

More intriguing are some of the intellectual references. Thus an observation on the Gorbachevs' first visit to Chequers. "Our advice at this time was that Mrs. Gorbachev was a committed, hardline Marxist; her obvious interest in Hobbes' *Leviathon,* which she took down from the shelf in the library, might possibly have confirmed that." Yes, there is an arguable affinity between the low view of human nature on which Hobbes predicated his analysis and the remorseless materialism of Marxist doctrine (if not always of Marx himself). In whose mind, though do we glimpse the recognition of such an affinity in this anecdote?

At another point we are invited to stand back from an argument over control of the television networks. "To use Benthamite language," Thatcher writes, "the public broadcasters were claiming the rights of poetry but providing us with pushpin." Does she normally use Benthamite language? A final example comes from her comments on the bicentennial of the French Revolution. "For me as a British Conservative, with Edmund Burke the father of Conservatism and the first great perceptive critic of the Revolution as my ideological mentor, the events of 1789 represent a perennial illusion." Again, this is not an obtuse or pretentious point in itself but it would be foolhardy to build too much on it without knowing whether it spontaneously occurred to the ostensible author to put it quite this way.

In one sense, it does not matter who actually wrote what, page by page or paragraph by paragraph. No more than Churchill did Thatcher draft every word published in her name. Yet this is still her book, created by a team whom she superintended and by methods similar to those which produced most of her public utterances. The central claims of the book and its tone are undoubtedly hers.

What she argues (or asserts, usually) comes as no great surprise. This is her apologia, not her apology, to the British people. "We have ceased to be a nation in retreat," she proclaimed in 1982. "We have instead a newfound confidence — born in the economic battles at home and tested and found true, 8,000 miles away." The Falklands episode, which so notably revived her political fortunes, is now distant in years as well as miles, and its rationale as well as its economic linkages may seem less transparently obvious to many people today. It was nonetheless the moment of truth for Thatcher's political leadership. She was subsequently taken at her own valuation and she subsequently felt an unshakable confidence in her own judgment, which she was ready to back against all comers.

She admits that she was not an easy colleague. But then, how could she be? "Of course, in the eyes of the 'wet' Tory establishment, I was not only a woman, but 'that woman', someone not just of a different sex, but of a different class, a person with an alarming conviction that the values and virtues of middle England should be brought to bear on the problems which establishment consensus had created." One can sympathize with her point of view, but also, perhaps, with the feelings of loyal colleagues who bore the brunt of her pent-up frustrations and her implacable self-righteousness. She now recognizes that her handling of Sir Geoffrey Howe — "I may, myself, have been less than tactful" — left something to be desired. This was to prove an expensive mistake in the long run.

Thatcher admits at one point that, "as I often did in government, I was using public statements to advance the arguments and to push reluctant colleagues further than they would otherwise have gone." When she says that she does "not believe that collective responsibility is an interesting fiction, but a point of principle," this is plainly how the principle must be understood to work in practice. Thatcher's conviction politics were inspired by the conviction that she was in the right.

These memoirs betray little sense that there was another side to the argument. More than that, the purity of her own intentions is persistently contrasted with the unworthy motivation of her opponents. There is something chilling about this routine disparagement, years after the heat of the contest has ceased to license it. Thus, the Liberal-Social Democratic Party Alliance campaign in 1987 was "marred by splits and that basic incoherence which is the nemesis of people who eschew principle in politics." Likewise, addressing the problems of poverty which remained under Thatcherism, "it was a cynical ploy for the Left to start talking as if they were old-fashioned Tories, fighting to preserve decency amid social disintegration." Thus she "never forgot that the unspoken objective of socialism — municipal or national — was to increase dependency. Poverty was not just the breeding ground of socialism; it was the deliberately engineered effect of it."

Here was a prime minister who was not hobbled by inner doubts — a highly effective mindset in a politician, and one to which many of her achievements can no doubt be attributed. But here, more unnervingly, is someone apparently a stranger to any sense of relativism, irony or magnanimity. She always knew best. Hence the paradox of a government whose rhetoric was often self-consciously libertarian, enforcing centralist solutions which faithfully reflected the prime minister's wild streak of moral authoritarianism.

The scheme for a national curriculum in state schools must be seen in this light. Look at these two successive sentences: "The fact that since 1944 the only compulsory subject in the curriculum in Britain had been religious education reflected a healthy distrust of the state using central control of the syllabus as a means of propaganda. But that was hardly the risk now: the propaganda was coming from left-wing local authorities, teachers and pressure groups, not us." The bland pluralism of the first sentence is immediately undercut by the one-eyed prejudice of the second.

This same mindset played a part in fomenting the policy which was arguably her undoing. It was her conviction about the poll tax which led her to designate it the flagship of her third term in office; it was her confidence in her own political judgment which led her to override the misgivings of her colleagues; and it was her unassailable sense of tutelary rectitude which governed her handling of the issue. The actual phrase "poll tax" is never uttered, of course; long after everyone else has succumbed to common usage, Thatcher persists in referring only to the "community charge." Nor will she admit now that it was misconceived; instead she reiterates that it could have worked, indeed was already working and, above all, that had her party kept its nerve, "I could have ridden through the difficulties."

Now the great argument for the poll tax was that it made local government accountable to local electors. Thus is provided a radical solution to the problem of local government overspending. This could now be left to the voters themselves to sort out, rather than subjected to interventionist measures of rate-capping from the centre. That is what Nicholas Ridley, the most loyal Thatcherite in cabinet, thought was at stake. Thatcher is unrepentant, not only of her general defence of the poll tax proposals, but of "pressing for much more extensive community charge capping than was ever envisaged for the rates." The explanation is simply that "I felt we needed this safeguard."

Thatcher's relations with Nigel Lawson, when he succeeded Howe as Chancellor, were a more equal battle of wits and will. Lawson insisted on playing his cards close to his chest, whereupon "Treasury spies, realizing that this was an impossibly secretive way of proceeding with someone who after all was 'First Lord of the Treasury,' furtively filled me in — with the strictest instructions not to divulge what I knew — before Nigel proudly announced to me his budget strategy." If this was the position during the heyday of the Thatcher-Lawson economic miracle, it is not difficult to credit the strains that were to develop in Downing Street when the going got rough.

It is at this stage in the book, in the aftermath of Thatcher's third election victory, that a new note is sounded. The story of the national curriculum introduces another vocabulary: "ran into difficulties ... never envisaged ... unfortunately ... next problem ... disappointing ... unsatisfactory ... very concerned ... appalled ... comprehensively flawed ... thoroughly exasperated ... very different from that which I originally envisaged."

Kenneth Baker carries the can here, and Chris Patten in the next section on housing policy, where the conclusion is: "The inertia of the DoE (Department of the Environment) had won out in the end." After this, it is little surprise to find that Lawson is repeatedly blamed for the overheating of the economy, which led to a resurgence of inflation after 1987, thus compromising the central claim of Thatcherite econ-omic competence. "In politics there are no final victories," we are told.

The final betrayal, personal as well as political, is already on the cards. Incidental causes of exasperation give way to chronic crises. Lawson and Howe cease to be irritating and become intolerable instead. Lawson's decision to leave the Treasury in 1989 remains incomprehensible, at least to Thatcher; a year later, Howe's decision that he had had enough at the Foreign Office "turned out to be almost a rerun of Nigel Lawson's resignation." Funny coincidence, that.

Heseltine's persistent disloyalty was soon to be eclipsed by Howe's "final act of treachery." The crisis of 1989 had been solved by drafting in Major as Chancellor, despite Thatcher's obvious misgivings. The crisis of 1990 gave him the premiership, to Thatcher's personal chagrin, but in the comfort that her ideological heritage was apparently secure. Her principles would surely endure. "The arguments for them seemed to me to have been won," she writes in hindsight. "I now know that such arguments are never finally won."

Margaret Thatcher's memoirs are a continuation of politics by other means. They have already done wonders for her bank balance; what they will do for her historical reputation is the real bottom line.

BRAD OVENELL-CARTER

Brad is living proof of the potential effect of gender stereotyping with small children. His mother — clearly a woman ahead of her time — apparently passed up the Mechano set one Christmas in favour of an Easy Bake Oven and Brad has been cooking ever since.

Raised in Richmond and educated at the University of British Columbia, Brad stepped into the market with an Education degree at a time when there was an unprecedented glut of teachers. He drifted quickly into the hospitality industry and soon worked his way up to head chef at an exclusive restaurant in Ottawa, where he and his wife Julie had moved while she pursued her Journalism degree. Returning to B.C., he worked in hotel and restaurant management before turning to food writing full time. He is the former food editor of *Vancouver* magazine and a frequent contributor to *Canadian Living* and *Western Living,* from which the following article is reprinted.

He and Julie moved to Bowen Island in 1989, at a time when they were just starting a family and seeking refuge from the city. They now have two children, Kathryn, 6, and Adam, 3.

Play
Dough

Ever since some discriminating Egyptian pyramid builder opened his lunchbox, took a mouthful of his sandwich and decided that the flat-bread lacked a certain *je ne sais quois*, no tinier bit of biology has provided humans with greater comfort than *Saccharomyces exiguus*. Yeast for short. While grain boiled to a thick paste and baked dry on a hot stone might have satisfied the belly, leavened bread, with its crackly crust and sculptural possibilities, satisfies the senses.

Aha, some clever wag among you will be saying: baker's yeast is in fact *Saccharomyces cerevisae*, not *S. exiguus!* But I have tricked you into revealing the point of my story.

Exiguus is the wild yeast used by the ancients and by moderns such as Lionel Poilâne in his world-famous *pain levain naturel* and by Steve Sullivan, in the sourdough that thousands of Bay Area residents deem good enough to rise at dawn and line up for. It is also the yeast I spent the last three years cultivating in my own kitchen.

My wife, Julie, has a fondness for sourdough bread and I had promised her a miracle of loaves: from nothing more than flour and water and a little salt, I told her, I shall create the life that renders dough into handsome rounds of thick-crusted loaves with a crackly bite that yield noisily to the gnash of teeth; a crumb that is creamy, moist and chewy; a flavour, ancient and earthy, recalling toasted wheat and tangy fermentation; an aroma hinting at more elusive things — roasted nuts, butterscotch, dried pears, grassy fields — that emanate from neither water, nor flour nor salt, but from some more mysterious source.

And that is what consumed me for the past three years, which may seem a long time, but in the history of breadmaking it is but a hiccup. According to Harold McGee in his comprehensive book *On Food and Cooking*, archaeological evidence favours the Egyptians as the happy discoverers that grain paste left for a few days will gather wild yeasts from the air, causing the dough to ferment. Professor Raymond Clavel, in his definitive *La Boulanger moderne*, places the earliest naturally leavened bread *"chez les Hébreux au temps des Môise."* My own sourdough adventure began much more recently.

TUESDAY, JUNE 11, 1991

To make sourdough, I will first need to make a starter, or chef, as Poilâne calls it. This is the piece of soft dough in which wild yeasts and lactic acid bacteria live in happy symbiosis, generating the gases, alcohols and acids that give sourdough its complex taste and chewy texture. Commercial yeasts produce clouds of carbon dioxide for a speedy rise, but at the expense of other aromatic compounds.

Unfortunately, when it comes to finding a bacterial source, I have almost nothing to go on. The three recipes I collect suggest the dubious addition of mashed potatoes or even bananas as a source of microbes, both of which I am reluctant to use. The Egyptians certainly didn't use potatoes, since no one had yet brought any back from the New World, and Julie hates bananas.

WEDNESDAY, JUNE 12

I contact a French chef and friend who says I need to get my hands on a copy of *Faire son pain*, a lucid treaty on naturally leavened bread by his countryman, Poilâne. I dial up the bookstore and am told my order will take at least two weeks.

I stall Julie with scientific obfuscation: yeasts are a group of single-celled fungi; about 160 different species are known — *S. cerevisae* is the one commonly used in baking and beer brewing, but *S. exiguus* is the one we're hunting for in sourdough. Sugars are the raw material that these yeasts convert into carbon dioxide and alcohol as normal products of their metabolic process. Grabbing a piece of paper and a pencil, I explain the equation:

$$C_6H_{12}O_6 \rightarrow 2C_2H_5OH + 2CO_2$$

"Great," she says, less impressed than I think she should be. "Does this mean I'll have sourdough soon?"

"Naturellement," I reply, exhausting my French just as fast as I had my knowledge of chemistry.

THAT AFTERNOON

Patience is a virtue but impatience gets things done. Harold McGee says American gold miners, the rough guys who invented San Francisco sourdough, made their starters by mixing flour and water and letting it spontaneously ferment. If the men who moiled for gold managed it on the trail, it should work in my kitchen. So I make a wad of dough about the size of a tennis ball, using 100 grams of unbleached flour and enough water to make a soft dough. I kneed this on my maple cutting board for two minutes, place it into a glass bowl, cover with a damp cloth, secure the cloth around the bowl's rim with butcher's twine and go about my business while waiting for Poilâne's book to arrive.

THURSDAY, JUNE 13

My starter smells like wet flour, nothing more. Maybe I've failed.

FRIDAY, JUNE 14

There is a sandy skin on the starter and it is definitely swollen; I can see tiny bubbles through the sides of the bowl. It seems early to declare success, but I am ecstatic. I telephone Vancouver baker Chris Brown, the most fanatical man I know bread-wise, and ask what to do next. Brown has wild yeast starters cultivating in his bakery, *Ecco Il Pane,* but dares not use them. He warns me that playing with wild yeasts is like playing with dynamite. Compared to bread leavened with commercial yeast, naturally leavened bread is slow, unpredictable, and prey to variations in flour, water, temperature, humidity — your first batch of sourdough can take six days from start to finish.

Italians refer to starter as a "wild horse," because there is no knowing when a batch will act up on its own and do whatever it pleases, sizzling and seething over the counter in violent life and filling the kitchen with a sour broccoli stink. Don't expect success on your first go, Brown warns me. He then instructs me to double the volume of dough, which I do by adding 100 grams of flour and room-temperature water a spoonful at a time to make a very soft dough. I place it in a bigger bowl and cover it again, using a clear shower cap.

As a way of limbering up, I have for several days been engaged in an intense bout of regular breadmaking, using a starter made from hazelnut-sized pieces of fresh compressed yeast, which I buy from the bakery department of the local supermarket. Brown says using this for your starter, which Italians call *biga,* approximates the practice of leavening today's bread with a piece of risen dough held over from yesterday's batch.

Julie shows fading tolerance for the fine dusting of flour covering every horizontal surface in the kitchen and which now threatens to drift into the rest of the house. I explain that breadmaking at home is, like most frugalities, penny wise and pound foolish. What it saves in money, it costs in time and cleanup duties. But it does aim at excellence, and as long as it gives good bread, its minor extravagances can hardly be faulted. For good measure, I take Julie away for the weekend.

SUNDAY, JUNE 16 — EARLY EVENING

It's alive! The starter has tripled, maybe quadrupled in volume and is pressing hard against its plastic cover. It smells tangy, somewhere

77

between beer and yóghurt. Large bubbles proudly show themselves through the glass. There can be no doubt about it: I have created life in a bowl in my kitchen.

I send Julie to bed and begin building my starter into a kilo of bread dough by dissolving it in 250 grams of water and working in 500 grams of flour and 15 grams of salt. Bakers weigh everything because flour can be packed loosely or densely in a measuring cup and doughs can be tight or aerated: it's their weight that matters.

The kneading begins. This is the process that aerates the dough and creates the millions of tiny pockets for the yeast to fill with carbon dioxide. It also unkinks the protein molecules into a miraculous elastic web that gives the bread its structure while stretching and expanding around the bubbles of carbon dioxide.

In his book, McGee offers a lengthy analysis of this process, explaining that it is possible to overwork dough so that it breaks down and loses all elasticity. After 20 minutes of pushing my dough away from my body with the heel of my hand, folding it back towards myself, giving it a quarter turn, again and again and again, I am the only thing to break down.

Next I turn to Julia Child, Louise Bertholle and Simone Beck, following their procedure for forming a round loaf in *Mastering the Art of French Cooking*, rolling and stretching the satiny dough ball into four tight spherical packages. I lightly oil two black steel baking sheets with virgin olive oil, then dust them with corn meal and set the loaves onto them, rough side down. Then to create a moist, draftless environment — ideal proofing conditions — I slide both baking sheets into a big green garbage bag and inflate it by bunching up the opening and blowing in my own hot air. My loaves will rise until midnight.

MIDNIGHT

A disappointing show — the loaves have barely risen by half, though they are suppose to have doubled. I decide to wait two more hours.

2 A.M.

Hardly any change in the loaves, but I put them in the oven, preheated to 500°F, anyway. Child and Beck say to use a razor blade to slash a decorative pattern on top of each loaf. Brown says to use a bread knife. I cut tic-tac-toe patterns using both and decide to stick to the knife in the future. Before closing the oven door, I douse the loaves with water from a spray bottle to delay the setting of the crust, thus trying to get maximum rise, or what bakers call "oven spring" from my bread.

2:03 A.M.

Another spray.

2:06 A.M.

Another spray.

2:20 A.M.

The loaves have not sprung as much as I would have liked and my slashes have remained as deep valleys, but I lower the heat to 400°F to let the bread brown, now that the crust is well set.

3:00 A.M.

My first sourdough is done! Aficionados everywhere swear bread tastes best when it has cooled and the complex flavours have had a chance to develop. Italy once had a law which forbade bakers to sell bread still warm from the oven. Unable to resist, I try a slice anyway. It has a thick, crunchy crust, a powerful tang, but the crumb is rather dense. Still I am not disappointed. I go to bed with crumbs on my smiling lips. Just for a moment I think of waking Julie, but if there is one thing she enjoys more than sourdough, it is her sleep.

THREE YEARS LATER

My six-year-old daughter and I have established a routine of baking bread every second day. The loaves have steadily improved in shape and density and the flavour has mellowed; sometimes we eat nothing else. I have had to make several new starters as each one has, as warned, become a wild horse and run away from me. Once I went to a health food store and bought a sack of organic flour with the idea that the fungicides sprayed on regular wheat might inhibit the development of wild yeasts. It was far too reactive and unpredictable to use again. Interestingly, even with regular unbleached flour the taste of our bread would change dramatically from one batch to the next as the various strains of yeast in the starter competed for dominance.

Sometimes it's tempting to break my breadmaking habit. It's too consuming, like having a pet. When we're away on vacation, I have to ask someone to come in and feed my starter by stirring in a little flour and water and I ask myself, is it worth it? But then I take out a label that I have trimmed from some store-bought bread:

Ingredients: enriched flour, water, sugar, sesame seeds, yeast, vegetable oil, shortening, salt, dextrose, contains potato flour or wheat gluten, mono and diglycerides, sodium stearoyl-2-lactylate, calcium sulphate, calcium propionate, calcium phosphate monobasic.

Our bread starts with just flour, water, salt. It's the kind of bread we can eat forever, and sometimes do.

MARIA TIPPETT

Maria Tippett found fame and acclaim in 1979 when she won the Governor-General's award for her definitive biography of *Emily Carr*. But her career as an academic, historian, curator and writer stretches off handsomely in either direction from that date.

In addition to her nine books, she is a frequent contributor to such publications as the *London Review of Books* and the *Times Literary Supplement*. She has taught at Simon Fraser University, the University of British Columbia and York University in Toronto and she is now a member of the Faculty of History at Cambridge University, where she and her husband, historian Peter Clarke, keep a second home.

Even before moving to Bowen Island in 1983, Tippett had kept a cottage on Mayne Island, from which she made her first foray into fiction with *Breaking the Cycle, and other stories from a Gulf Island*. She is currently working on another collection called *Berlin Stories* from which the following contribution is taken.

Going
the
Wrong Way

Suddenly the prop jet was racing down the runway, lifting off the tarmac, folding up its wheels, and cutting a wide arc over the city. The passengers were silent during the first few airborne minutes. But when the aircraft had gained altitude, pointed its nose eastward and Schoenefeld airport had mingled with the rest of the urban sprawl, everyone relaxed, began chatting, shifted their ample bodies in their tiny seats, lit cigarettes and foraged in their carry-on bags for food. For who knew what awaited them by way of refreshment upon their arrival in Moscow?

The first hour of the flight was uneventful. A small, spare man clung to the sloping sill of a plastic-framed window and muttered half to himself and half to the lady towering beside him: *"Das habe ich zu fuss getan?"* The big lady did not share the man's amazement that he'd walked all the way from Berlin to the outskirts of Moscow and back again because she was rumaging through her handbag.

She wasn't searching for something to eat or for cigarettes, but for papers. Yellow, brittle, crease-ridden papers informing her that more than 45 years earlier she, Katie Schultz, would be a widow for the rest of her life because Hauptman Werner Schultz had fallen in Poland.

This hadn't happened during the harsh winter of 1941-1942 when the Barbarossa campaign was revealed for all its folly. But at the war's end. When every other German survivor of the 153 divisions that had invaded Russia was retreating, Hauptmann Schultz had headed East. He'd reached his destination — a small village on the Vistula River — taken charge of his fallen comrades' motley, frost-bitten regiment, then promptly died from the cold, from starvation, or perhaps from the sheer exhaustion of having walked all the way there.

It was a common story. The East was a void into which young and old, good and bad had disappeared throughout the war. Even those soldiers who were unfortunate enough to be Russian when peace was declared were rounded up, put into camps, where most of them perished. *"Druben," "im Osten"* or *"im Russland Gefallen"* were euphemisms for death, for what Kristallnacht, the annexations of Poland, Czechoslovakia and Austria, along with so many other terrible things, had led.

Katie hadn't been at all surprised when the notice came. It was a relief. It put an end to her state of uncertainty. It calmed her shattered nerves. She had even been able to garner a morsel of comfort from the knowledge that Werner had died above and beyond the line of duty. For Hauptmann Schultz's death had not been a commonplace event. It differed from the deaths of the men whose widows Katie met at the Zentral graveyard when every Christmas and Easter they placed artificial wreaths, cut flowers and sturdy plants on to coffinless graves. Hauptmann Schultz's death had been — how did the telegram put it, Katie wondered as she adjusted her rimless glasses and lifted the paper towards her pale blue eyes — it had been valiant. She allowed the sound of the word to ring in her head. Then she traced its physical properties by mouthing it silently to herself. But any attempt to bring it to life was interrupted by the rattling aircraft and by the little man's continuous assertion that he'd not only walked all the way to Moscow but back again too.

The man wasn't boasting. He was simply marvelling at the fact that during the course of the next two-and-a-half-hours he would cover a distance that had taken him weeks to traverse in shoes that were not fit for walking and in clothes that were not thick enough to withstand the weather past the month of October.

Katie caught the full meaning of the man's pronouncement and looked down. He was small, wiry and not much past seventy. He was so unlike Werner who'd been heavy — some might have even called him fat — but not heavy enough to ward off the cold. Couldn't have been an officer, Katie thought. Couldn't have been in charge of a company of men: too young, too wiry, not enough presence.

Werner's position had brought unimagined status to the Schultz family. Like his father and his father before him Werner had cast, then glued, then painted decorative plaster of Paris mouldings onto the ceilings and walls of vast Berlin apartments. It had been a demanding job with long hours, difficult-to-please customers and little pay. His entry into the Wehrmacht in 1938, his rise to lieutenant in 1939, then to captain a year later had changed all of this. Officer rank gave Werner a car and a driver, provided Katie with luxuries when few were to be had, and introduced them both to a circle of congenial friends.

Katie was uneasy with her new-found status. In order to avoid putting on airs before the neighbours she instructed the driver to wait around the corner of the apartment block when he called to take her to parties. Once there, when people gathered around the piano — for dancing was forbidden and someone always played the piano — and sipped from tall crystal glasses of champagne — which for some strange reason was plentiful throughout the war — Katie held back. She stood on the fringe of the semicircle, drank no more than one glass of champagne, and watched every word and gesture lest she embarrass Werner before his fellow officers and their wives. Boisterous, hail-fellow-well-met, Werner provided a shield behind which Katie hid her shyness.

She had only taken advantage of Werner's position once. It was early in 1944 during the worst months of the bombing. Night after night their love-making, their valued time together was interrupted by sounds, by vibrations, by the smell of gas mixed with rust and rubble, and by their own terror which saw them scurrying down three flights of stairs to a damp basement for shelter. What Katie wanted and asked Werner to find her was a negligee. She'd never had one before; always preferred stiff linen high-necked sensible nightgowns that held in her emotions and hid the ample curves of her body. God only knows where Werner found the deep purple see-through affair that fell just below Katie's knees. She never asked. She was simply glad that one evening when the bombing had stopped long enough to allow them to transcend the smells and the fear of being buried alive, she'd been able to show Werner just how much she could please him. That evening, their last together, Katie Schultz cast modesty to the wind.

"What's taking you to Moscow?"

Katie started, blotted out the past to recover the present, and looked down. "I've always wanted to see the domed churches, the Bolshoi Ballet, the gold in the Kremlin, the monastery at Sagorsk, and Lenin's tomb" Katie lied as she rattled off the attractions that had been so nicely illustrated in Herti Department Store's glossy travel brochure.

"And you?" Katie asked as she slid the yellow papers back in to a secure place in her handbag.

"I'm looking forward to having a look at the city I missed 'visiting' in 1943," the man said as he chuckled and nodded towards the window. "I'm on my own now, retired, and have lots of time to travel."

And no doubt lots of money, too, Katie added to herself as she caught the glitter of the man's gold watchband peeking beneath the sleeve of his grey silk suit. It had taken Katie two years to save for her trip. She'd only thought of making it after hearing that many of the other war widows at the Zentral cemetery had assembled their papers and headed East. What they did and found out once they got to Moscow Katie didn't know. But they all seemed happier after they came home.

Katie had saved for her trip by putting aside a few marks every month in a specially marked envelope. She was proud of her envelope system. It had enabled her to keep Werner's grave as nice as the others at the cemetery, to live in a decent one-bedroom apartment — though it was three floors up a steep flight of stairs — to have enough coal for the winter — each apartment had its own clay-tiled oven — and to eat one slice of cake with whipping cream on the side at the Kempinski Restaurant every afternoon. She'd begun her envelope system in the summer of 1945 when she'd taken the job, her first ever, as a cleaning lady.

Six days a week Katie walked from her room in the Hardenbergstrasse to a once-elegant building on the edge of the Tiergarten. The building had been seconded as living quarters for a rowdy, homesick, war-weary group of young Russian officers. The men needed a cleaning lady and Katie needed the job. The soldiers for whom she scrubbed, swept and tidied, defecated in the closets and washed their vegetables in the toilet bowl. And they might have made sexual advances if she had not faked a limp. It was a hideous limp. So ugly and twisted, so — "how can you possibly mount her" one of the soldiers had joked — that they left her alone. It was now that Katie's envelope system came into use and had been in use ever since.

"What with Glasnost, the wall coming down" — the man really did want to chat — "and the recognition of our homelands in the northwest of the Soviet Union, the Russians are becoming more friendly, more like us. Did you know that there is even new evidence to suggest that they weren't so bad to us during the war after all? Have you seen the latest issue of *Stern* magazine?"

Katie nodded and moved her legs to one side so that the man could locate the magazine from under his seat. She wasn't eager to read about the war. Her part in it had been played. She'd accepted the consequences. But the man insisted.

"Look at this article. It's about the American and British prisoner-of-war camps that were set up in the spring of 1945 throughout Germany. It says that all those stories about so many of us dying in the East are not true. It says that the numbers were faked by the Allies who wanted to retaliate against us, who hadn't the means to feed and house so many soldiers, and who wanted to make sure that we didn't go over to the East politically."

The man handed Katie the glossy magazine. Why should she bother to read it now? By the time she arrived home her copy would be under her doormat folded in half which annoyed her since she paid her neighbour for half the cost of the subscription. But one had to be polite. The man had been quiet up to now. And there was barely half an hour to go before landing.

Katie spread the magazine onto her ample lap. She licked her forefinger and turned to the feature article.

"They were not given rations, bedding, or shelter. And because they had no status as soldiers the Red Cross were forbidden to assist them."

Katie read on. Apparently trainloads of food had been stopped at the Swiss-German border. She turned the page. A map of a much larger Germany indicated where the camps had been with small black crosses. There were camps that she'd never heard of before. Camps that were not camps at all but parcels of land surrounded by coils of barbed wire. There was even a cross marked on the outskirts of Berlin. And, on the following page, a large black-and-white photograph featuring one section of it. The ground looked parched. Must have been taken during the rainless summer of 1945. The summer when Katie got the notice of Werner's death. The summer she applied for the plot at the cemetery and got it. The summer she took the cleaning job. And the summer she sold the purple negligee on the black market in order to buy food.

"There was no water, no sanitation, not even proper shelter" the caption under the photograph read.

The men in the photograph stood or sat beside tiny caves they had carved out of the dry summer earth with their tin cups. Beyond the wire that separated them from the open fields were women wearing scarfs. Some were pushing bread through the tangled mass of wire. Others were just watching: one hand on hip, the other cupped over their mouth in disgust, to avoid the stench, or for whatever reason Katie didn't know. She turned the page and continued reading: "Most of the prisoners starved. Their bodies were thrown into mass graves."

"Well, what do you think of that, interesting eh?"

Katie had to agree. It gave the whole business a new twist. While agreeing she turned back to the photograph of the camp on the outskirts of Berlin. She scanned the faces of the soldiers and caught the profile of a large man dressed in the tattered remnants of a field officer's uniform. He was sitting beside a hovel, elbows on knees, hands clasp together, head titled slightly to one side. Katie stared so intensely at the photograph that after a while all she saw were the small black and grey dots that made it up. But when she pulled the magazine away from her nose and allowed her eyes to focus there was no mistake. It was Werner. Werner alive in the summer of 1945. Werner living on the same side of Berlin a mere tram's ride from the Hardenbergstrasse.

Katie tried to stand up but the seat belt cut a fold in her stomach. She fumbled for the clasp; the metal felt cool against her sweating palm.

When it finally snapped and she was able to stand up the small man unbuckled his seat belt too. He retrieved the magazine which had slid off Katie's lap to the floor. Assuming that the big woman wanted to powder her nose before landing, he placed the tips of his fingers on the ledge of the plastic window frame and resumed looking out. By the time he was lost in thought, back on the outskirts of Moscow, Katie had made her way to the back of the plane where two stewardesses were having a surreptitious cigarette before preparing their passengers for the landing.

When Katie approached, their smoking hands disappeared behind their backs. And when Katie shouted "I'm going the wrong way, I don't want to go to Moscow after all," they looked bewildered. They hadn't been taught how to deal with someone who wanted to get off an aircraft before it had landed. There had been those who had got on the wrong flight and after an hour's ride had found themselves in the wrong city. But this was different. This woman knew where she was going but had suddenly changed her mind, decided that she didn't want to go to Moscow after all, and wanted to get off. And the woman looked so determined, so red-faced, so angry and frustrated at the same time that they didn't know what to do.

But the young women didn't have to do anything because the captain suddenly asked all passengers to return to their seats and Katie, who always followed orders, turned round. As she made her way up the narrow corridor she began to limp and twist. It was a hideous limp. So ...

TERESA PLOWRIGHT

Teresa Plowright is staking out new ground in science fiction literature, setting provocative psychological dramas in science fiction trappings. The effect is remarkable, if sometimes unsettling. Readers are inclined to treat the story as fantasy and let down their guard, only to be drawn into an intricate plot that shows that human foibles and frailties remain consistent, whether the players are cast in Shakespeare or Star Trek.

Plowright's first novel *Dreams of an Unseen Planet,* was published in Canada, the U.S. and England and her second, tentatively titled *Natural Instinct,* is due out in November, 1994. She has also written numerous short stories and screenplays and is working on a children's book called *Catlantis.*

All this literary output is relegated to the dark hours past midnight, given that her other job is raising three boys under the age of seven. Plowright and husband Russell Wills came to Bowen Island almost six years ago in search of a community in which children were cherished: "We knew the minute we got off the ferry that this was it for us."

Making History

1 Lyon

"So here you are, your first trip Topside..." Lyon ushered his old pal into a sumptuous bar. "Just to visit little ol' me?" He grinned disbelievingly.

Wakefield was having trouble walking; the floor, like the walls of the Black Diamond Lounge, was clear, and below his feet the universe fell away forever into black and stars. Under the grand piano floated the heart-stopping pendant of blue-green Earth. "I could never afford a trip to moonstation just for pleasure. There's something important I came about."

Lyon ordered drinks from a bleached-blond Asian, then gazed outside at the mammoth interplanetary craft in their cargo bays, outward bound into space so vast and dark ... "You know, it's weird," Lyon half-whispered, "this must-go-down-to-the-sea thing I get."

"Lyon ..." Wakefield whispered back, "I've got 200 people who want to sail away on one of those."

Lyon giggled. "You're crazy, man! Even here on moonstation, we can hardly offer enough booze and other amenities to fill two shifts." Lyon was a personnel procurement officer; he should know.

Wakefield sipped his Stellar Zowie before he spoke. "You've heard of terraforming, haven't you?"

Making a cratered desert bloom ... First, a siege of rockets (—

obsolete, dirt-cheap), would bomb Saturn's small, dead moon with chemicals, to start the Warm — freeing water locked in polar caps, melting ancient permafrost, swaddling an atmosphere around the cold lump, so that bacteria could start the swarm of life ...

Lyon shelled peanuts onto the celestial floor. "Like what the UN is doin' on Mars."

"Right! But we — my people — will do it 10 times as fast." In just a dozen years the Frontierists would sally forth, and set up gas-maker factories, so that soon low-oxygen ancient plants like horsetails could be grown, and rotted richly into soil, and then, with fertilizer from human beings —

"Who's we?" Lyon squinted. "Some weird Dissenter group?"

"No! Just ordinary people, like me — fed up with home! Just imagine, Lyon: we'll take genestocks for flowers, butterflies; there could even be leopards — elephants!" His shy blue eyes willed Lyon: See our dream!

Lyon ruffled Wakefield's pale, longish hair, shaved to make the forehead extra high. "Hey Wake, you been in the ivory tower too long. Gov'ment won't ever okay that scheme."

Wakefield looked out to the cargo bays, and gnawed his lip. "Let's just say — we've got an angle on government. What I need now is a ship that we can outfit with 200 cryoberths."

Lyon snorted. "You ordinary people must be filthy rich."

"No, we're not." The blue eyes were plain and sad. "To get the money — I'll put it this way: we've got to sell half our dream to someone else. Someone I truly can't talk about."

Lyon shrugged. "We-e-e-ell ... I know one freelancer might re-fit, for the proper sum."

When he named a figure, Wakefield winced. "Look ..." he muttered, feeling soiled holding out a bribe, "if you can keep the cost down — we'll make it worth your while."

Lyon, however, beamed right back, and with the finances clarified happily bought more rounds. Wakefield was wobbly when he finally rose to leave, and heard his slurred voice ask, "Lyon — why don't you come home any more?"

"Hey, I get a buzz from the Bop, like everyone. Oh yeah!" Lyon's eyes drifted out to the black silence. "I do plan to get down home. Real soon."

II Elsbeth

Wakefield retrieved his car at Pegasus Terminal and after an hour in the usual heat had nosed out of the vast Terminal lot and into the Bop freeway that snaked from L.A. to The Bay. Once past the lot's guard-house he picked up a jockey, one of the bits of human flotsam ("grunts", Lyon would call them), who earned a few newdols taking cars through traffic snarls. This kid's feet hardly reached the pedals.

"You sure you know how to drive?" Wakefield asked.

"Sure, boss," he nodded: brown skin, brown eyes; asian-indo-mexi-can? "Can."

A moment later, he peered at Wakefield. "No TV, boss?"

All up and down the river of cars, tiny built-ins in the dashboards were tuned into the teleromanas beamed over half the globe by satellite from Brazil, where they did them best. "Eduardo," a sultry heroine in a bedroom would bare her breasts, "we mustn't do this."

When the car moved too fast, the safety-mech cut the picture off; but it hardly mattered what got lost. What counted was the fix of emo-tion: "Carissima —" the small flickering hero undid his shirt, "At last!"

Oh, there was no doubt that Wakefield wanted out of all this. When he and Lyon had been diving pals, they'd joked that the ocean floor was the world's last quiet place. Montana served more cappuccino than Italy, treks in Canada cost a leg, and L.A. pulsed with float-cantons.

"Hey, boss," the jockey reached gently toward the radio, "some music, nuh?" This frail little grunt fit in far better than Wakefield; live in the Bop, get into its buzz.

The phone was in Wakefield's hand to dial; he pictured Elsbeth in her university office cubbyhole with its musty history books, pushing back her reddish hair with impatience (hair shaved high at the forehead, as his was), willing her phone to ring with news. "He thinks he can do it," he told her at once.

She expelled a breath. "Thank god. And I suppose," she added with a nervous laugh, "he thinks we're nuts to share our utopia with a crazy cult? I know you told him, Wakefield."

(And of course, he had; Lyon's hoot had startled the Diamond Lounge. "The Oversoul Pan-Gi!" he'd guffawed. "Maybe you forgot, Wake — that guy is dead! Three clones, what an ego," Lyon had clucked, and philosophized: "You know, that whole cloner stuff was sick, dealers wanting to breed whores and slaves ... You know ..." he'd finished with a lopsided grin, "Downside is kind of a shitty world.")

"So," Elsbeth's voice continued, as the traffic snaked, "You'll be meeting with our illustrious partners soon?"

"I'm stopping by the Alliance — now."

"Now! It'll be past midnight when you get home. Oh, I know." Her voice went tight. "A personal relationship is a small sacrifice to make for a whole new world."

"Elsbeth, please …" He knew that she was as committed to the dream as he was, but she deplored Wakefield's clever scheme that had made the starry-eyed imaginings of a group of discontented academics suddenly, pragmatically, feasible. The scheme that had catapulted Wakefield into leadership, so that now, so very improbably, he was cutting deals with the Pan-Gi's cult, with Lyon, with Government …

Strange new pressures tweaked behind his high pale forehead, as the car inched down the shimmering freeway, toward the Oversoul Alliance headquarters.

"I don't mind sacrificing for the migration, Wakefield." A pleading entered Elsbeth's voice that she tried to laugh away. "I'm only saying that I want to start our new life with you — not lose you somewhere on the way."

"Elsbeth — I'll be home as soon as I possibly can," he said, and hung up; and brooded, until the car pulled into a sudden oasis of trees. He tossed the jockey an extra newdol as the kid jumped out: "Stay cool," Wakefield advised; and the small face grinned, as the thin brown legs pumped back toward the sunset plain of cars.

III The Guardians

It was in fact only Wakefield's second meeting with the OverSoul Alliance Guardians, who were shepherding the flock in the Gi's absence.

As the day's heat loosened up at last, he took a seat on a wrought-iron chair in the famous Garden that could only be called paradisical. A handful of men of various hues, all clad in purple robes, faced him around a glittery tabletop. "I can get a ship," he reported with shy pride. "And on your side — have you got the approvals yet?"

The Guardian named Caspar answered (pale hands folded neatly on a tummy paunch, in the body language of lifelong affluence). "We've had … unofficial assurances."

"Good as guaranteed," added a Guardian named Aloys (perhaps a former grunt, to judge by a scar on his cheek). "Gov'ment wants rid of the Gi's Sons bad."

Wakefield took a long draught of flowered air. "Then perhaps our dream comes true."

But no one else's expression looked relieved.

"Mr. Ottie," Caspar said soberly, "I think it's time you know a little more of us." Immediately, a white-robed acolyte set a machine onto the table; Caspar popped a holo button into place. "To begin with — I doubt very much you've ever seen the Gi."

Instantly a holo bobbed up of a sorrowful, joyful, dewy-eyed brown face (propaganda, Wakefield supposed, for potential converts, and he was intrigued; the Destabilizing Information Act severely curtailed all material about the Oversouls).

"Who am I?" The OverSoul Pan-Gi's holo intoned, and then giggled engagingly. "No simple question, for anyone. But even in the most superficial sense, I am a more confusing case than most." The Gi's voice was an exotic version of a British accent, with clipped consonants and strange dipthongs. 'Question' was 'quess-ti-on'.

"I am exactly a mix of everything. I am East meets West and goes back to both again."

Actually, Wakefield had learned a few facts about this mystery in the past few hectic weeks. Surinder Patel was the son of a poor West Indian woman in Trinidad (father a question mark) who'd worked as a daytime maid until, in a stroke of blinding luck, she'd married a reclusive British engineer whose house she'd been cleaning for just six weeks. Engineer Perkins had packed the family off to middle-class comfort in Malaysia.

Surinder, however (after years at an expensive American school culminating in a coveted degree in marketing), had, to his mother's hissing horror, flown off to study religion in India and might have become just one more ashram drifter had not some potent mix of influences gelled, sending him back to the U.S.A. at the age of 33.

"Thirty-three: just like the Christ-man," the Gi's bright-eyed face remarked. "The proper age for a prophet to begin to lead."

What exactly was the Gi's philosophy? The OverSoul (as the caramel face proclaimed) was The Great-One-Whom-No-One-Finds-by-Search; and perhaps because It was so limitless, the Gi didn't really dwell on It (or He or She). Not that this lessened his appeal.

"Here come the rich guys," Aloys, the olive-skinned Guardian with the scar, harumphed with what might have been humour, in the unclear dusk. "First, the Gi said it's okay to be filthy rich."

On a vast green lawn, the purple-robed Gi posed by a gazebo with a wealthy group. "If your lot is poverty," he preached, "you win great grace for a future life. If your lot is riches — live this fate with beauty." The Gi delighted in the heavily-guarded gardens of his moneyed friends:

"Making a garden," he said serenely, "cleans the soul."

Paradoxically, once he had a well-financed start, his popularity tore through the grunts. Perhaps it was his charismatic use of satellite; or perhaps reincarnation finally made some desperate sense to people with no earthly hope. But by then, the Gi had begun to change, because he was already ill, some claimed. But in any case, in the holos, his increasingly thin form made its way through squatters' sprawls and urban slums, and out of his speeches burst heartbreak: "My suffering kindred, my hopeless ones!"

"Amen!" said Aloys. "He's on track now."

But 'Hopeless ones'? When each earthly soul was supposedly recycling through endless existences? Suddenly the Gi poured money into shelters, schools for grunts …

"You deserve more" — his sobbing face shouted to a roaring crowd — "my hopeless ones!" Dissenters began to flock to him …

And Government hadn't been one bit pleased. Caspar cut off the holo with the Gi still in adoring crowds. "Well, you know the end of the story, Mr. Ottie."

"Bastards," Aloys said, with bitter grief, "stole his last few months." He withered the words: "Plane accident."

Wakefield nodded; that part of the story, everyone knew. And yet (whatever the fate of the Pan-Gi's soul), three flesh-and-blood progeny had been tucked into willing wombs, just before the new laws had outlawed clones.

"I don't suppose the story has really ended, though," Wakefield ventured. "The clones —"

"The Sons," Aloys corrected him.

"— can make a brand new start, on our colony."

White-haired Caspar rose. "Mr. Ottie … of course we too yearn to make a new biosphere: as He said, to make a garden cleans the soul. But you must understand: our most urgent goal is simply to get one Son out of Government's reach, alive."

"One Son! What about the other two?"

"Bastards!" Aloys swore again in a harsh low voice, while Caspar answered softly, "You surely know that Government has kept the Sons under house arrest for the past six years."

"For their own protection," another Guardian scoffed.

"The truth is," Caspar moved a little distance away, "that none of our sources has heard from Gi-Segundo for a long, long time. We still keep up hope … when Government schedules your interviews with the Sons, we would be elated if you meet with Segundo too."

Again Wakefield was startled. "Interviews?"

Caspar sighed. "Government is playing a very tough game with us.

No OverSoul follower will be allowed to see the Sons before the migration leaves — not the Guardians, not anyone. Rule number two: the migration must leave before the Sons turn 33."

"But, that's barely 10 years —"

Caspar swept his words aside. "And rule number three: only one Gi will go." Gesturing Wakefield into silence, he paced in the dusk. "Which Son, Mr. Ottie? Government won't choose, there'd be riots if it did. Nor would we want to decide, even if permitted — how could His followers choose among His Sons?"

Wakefield felt his chest tighten as Caspar stepped close. "As a pragmatic solution to an insoluble problem, Government thinks the choice should rest with your Frontierist group."

"But how can you agree to have just one Son go —"

Caspar's pouchy face went hard. "Obviously, we're cutting our losses, Mr. Ottie. Sacrificing one Son to save the other one."

Thus, on top of his other pressures, Wakefield would decide which Son would lead his people to a promised land.

V The Sons

Two days later, Wakefield followed a guard up a long driveway through a flower-bedded lawn, on the way to meet Tercero, with a joke of Lyon's drumming in his head: "It must feel just great to be guarded by Gov'ment, when Gov'ment's longing to see you dead."

Tercero's place of incarceration was a spacious home, with blossoms bright outside; but Wakefield found a withdrawn and monk-like youth, inside in the quiet of dim tiled rooms. Tercero was dressed in a plain white dhoti of coarse homespun.

"Have you seen Segundo yet?" he asked at once in a quiet voice; and when Wakefield shook his head, the young face grew pained. "They say he's dead. Have you heard that?"

What could he answer when the house was surely bugged? "I think there's some uncertainty ..."

The young Gi waved a hand at the walls. "I don't care in the slightest what they hear. And I've been told exactly why you've come." Wakefield nodded; he'd insisted that the Sons be fully briefed. "Well," Tercero went on, "I admire your vision; but I don't want to lead anybody anywhere."

Wakefield was confused: this physical replica of the long-dead Gi was profoundly disorienting — Tercero even had a mild form of his

95

father's drawl. Yet how could any clone of the Pan-Gi be a recluse?

"You see," the youth said with the composure of a much older man, "I've had a long, lonely time to consider my Father — also my identical Brother, speaking genetically — and to my way of thinking he was on the wrong path for most of his life." Tercero settled on a rush mat on the floor, ignoring the divan where Wakefield sat.

"Vaunting himself, surrounding himself with luxury ... Only almost too late did he try to use his monster organization to do some good. I love my Father, and I believe that he would have turned away from all his excesses — he was changing every day, when they slaughtered him. He would have withdrawn, lived simply — as he did during his years in India."

A flicker of longing came over Tercero's face. "That's where I want to go; but they won't let me. They'll never believe that I truly am no threat."

Ah! Suddenly the phenomenon made some sense. Wakefield was looking at certain heightened facets of the Pan-Gi's personality: certain traits in ascendance, now ... But which traits would dominate in 10 years time? The social scientist in Wakefield was mesmerized.

"But think about it!" he urged. "Wouldn't you like to live freely, instead of being a prisoner?"

The other laughed. "To most, this prison would be a paradise. Think of how the billions live!"

"But — what about the chance to make a better world? If you came with us, you wouldn't have to lead in the sense of giving orders — just be the figurehead, for the beginning years ..."

Wakefield launched into his vision, and slowly a considering alertness came over Tercero; and once Wakefield finally stopped, the brown face stayed cocked and questioning. Then the expression brightened so vividly that for a moment Tercero showed all the shine and twinkle of his famous sire. "Crazy Dreamer!" he shook a chiding finger at his guest, and laughed. "Just when I strive to deny all desire, to gain at least that blessing from my solitude — you come and want me to burn with your fever too!" He shook his head. "And do I have so weak a will, that indeed, indeed ... perhaps you have infected me with your dream?"

Abruptly, he stood up, and with a small, curt wave, he left the room. Wakefield waited awkwardly, thinking perhaps he'd been bid farewell; at last he stepped outside, and spied Tercero pacing underneath a vine-covered pergola. The young man strode over, and soberly looked Wakefield in the eyes. "This is my hour to meditate inside. I will make no sales-pitch to recommend myself. But if you want me in your migration, if you should choose me ... Yes, Mr. Wakefield Ottie, I would go."

Wakefield felt a surge of warmth as the slim fingers grasped his:

perhaps, at last, he'd found a true ally, for the mission that had brought such lonely pressures to his life.

• • •

He met Primero on the following afternoon — Primero, who looked so much like his brother Tercero that Wakefield felt squeamish: truly some law of nature had been mocked with these clones.

But unlike ascetic Tercero, Primero twinkled right from the start, sitting purple-robed in his own luxuriant garden-prison, brewing tea in a silver pot. "Come, Mr. Ottie, join me, please," he beckoned with a charming smile and an accent much more dramatic than Tercero's.

As if reading Wakefield's mind, he laughed. "You find I sound a little foreign for a chap raised in the U.S.A.? You see, all three of us modelled ourselves very closely on our Father in our early years. We all lived together in a special home attended by the most devoted OverSouls, and we saw holos of Father every night.

"We three Sons are very strange creatures, Wakefield — if I may call you that. Don't underestimate how odd we are." They sipped tea for a moment and then Primero beamed with a look of relaxed amusement. "I suppose Tercero told you he doesn't want to be a leader of men?"

Wakefield felt like he'd been pricked. "Why do you ask that?"

"Because I know a thing or two," Primero answered playfully. "Let me warn you, Wakefield, you must be very careful in interpreting whatever we Sons say. For one thing, our every word is listened to most attentively by Government ears. So there's perhaps a practical motive to proclaim in a hearty voice, 'Believe me, I'm no leader' — because a tame Gi wouldn't be a danger, hmmm?"

Wakefield nodded. "I see your point."

"But then, of course," Primero rose and strode around his little table, "there are other interpretations of us too, oh yes. Suppose," he stopped and cocked his head, "that Tercero were to feign a certain disinterest in your brain-child. You might find yourself persuading him of its merits — Ha! You might practically beg him to share your dream!"

Primero laughed, while Wakefield sipped tea uncomfortably. "Oh, Wakefield — " The First Son sat down again. "I'm afraid I'm a much cruder chap. I'll tell you frankly, I want the life my Father meant for me: to be a leader, surrounded by people that I can help! And to create a world — I was born for it, however odd my birth! So there you are, I've said my piece, no matter who hears; and you can interpret what you wish of me — and Tercero."

Then his face clenched painfully the way his brother's had. "You aren't seeing Segundo, are you?"

Wretchedly, Wakefield shook his head. "No, I knew you weren't. Because, you see, Segundo was the bravest and most outspoken of us all."

97

VI Caspar

Wakefield's life became an agony of questions: Which of the Sons would make the best Pan-Gi with whom to share a small new world? And which was he going to leave behind? Everyone was waiting for him to decide, the Frontierists, the Guardians ...

"Of course, the Alliance will try to protect whichever Son remains," Caspar told him during a private evening stroll, when Wakefield had driven to the Alliance Garden to find some calm.

"We'll apply what pressure we can on Government, brandish our usual big stick, the threat of mass protest if the Son is harmed ... but frankly, I doubt we could protest much, if Government did destroy the remaining Son."

Caspar clasped his hands behind himself and looked frank. "Mr. Ottie, many citizens were somewhat repulsed when the Pan-Gi cloned himself. The general public might feel that one surviving clone, sent off-planet, is quite enough. Any protests we made, might risk backlash."

In other words, Government could do as it pleased. And the Son who stayed behind was doomed.

"I can't do it, Elsbeth!" Wakefield sat up in bed, in the small gray hours; he'd lost the gift of sleep, while Elsbeth dozed lightly by his side, waiting for his fits of talk.

"I can't hold these two men's lives in my hands!"

"You do hold their lives, Wakefield. There's no point saying otherwise." She turned on the light. "What you really mean is, you can't decide."

"What if Tercero *was* trying to manipulate me, like Primero said? And then there's the problem about their youth ... In 10 years Tercero could be a flagrant hedonist, Primero might become selfless and serious ... How can I see that far ahead?"

"You have to decide which one is best for us. God forbid we should share that tiny world with some megalomaniac." Unvoiced was her deep reprimand that he'd ever involved 'that crazy cult'.

Mercifully, Wakefield reminded himself, the original Pan-Gi had never showed signs of psychosis. But what if the Sons had been warped in their short strange lives?

Day after day, he waded through psychological information that Government had compiled on each Son; but he found no help. Then, one morning, Lyon phoned: a call that must have taken a hefty bite from his profits for arranging the ship.

"Hey, Wake, just want to say: keep an empty place on that bus, okay? A reserved seat."

Wakefield's nerves were like flayed skin. "For God's sake, Lyon, we've got over 400 Frontierists who want 100 berths." What did Lyon want to do — sell the seat to get more money for cosmic drinks?

"Hey Wake," Lyon insisted affably, "you want that ship? Then you play ball with me. Hardball, Wake. The way the game is played, outside the ivory walls."

A game he should perhaps learn himself, Wakefield thought grimly after Lyon hung up: he was getting nowhere, being high-principled with everyone. Maybe he had to think differently …

"I've got an idea," he told Elsbeth that evening, instead of eating the dinner she'd just prepared. "I'm going to set up a kind of test! I'll bribe the guards, and get them to offer each Son the chance to arrange the death of the other one. Then we'll see if either one has a criminal potential or not."

Elsbeth sat down and bit her lip. "It's a bad idea."

"Why, for God's sake?" He felt he'd had a bold idea — this was leadership!

She went more pale. "Wakefield, when a person, especially someone naive like you, starts to plot, so many things can go wrong …" She gave him only vague protest, when he longed to be told anything with certainty.

Wakefield stormed to his car and drove once again to the OverSouls garden, where Caspar was waiting in the perfumed dusk, calm and patrician in his purple robe.

"I've got an idea." Wakefield repeated his plan, somewhat feverish from lack of sleep.

The sound of the cicadas buzzed and the relief he felt was dizzying when after a small silence, Caspar nodded assent. "It's an extraordinary measure," Caspar sighed, "but perhaps a necessity, if it enables you to finally make a choice."

"Then you think it can work?"

"With our help." He added, seeing Wakefield's protesting face, "You can hardly attempt to bribe the guards yourself. What if Government heard of it? You'd jeopardize the whole migration. Clearly, the only way to send your message to the Sons is through the Guardians. We have channels we know are safe."

Wakefield still looked troubled.

"Mr. Ottie — Wakefield — do you think that we, the Guardians, would want to participate in such a ruse? It's a terrible twist of fate, for us, the followers of the Pan-Gi, to deceive his Sons. But look at the situation." He held out his hands. "It's absolutely imperative that you make a choice: any choice, so that we can save one Son. And you're not able to. We must push history forward! Even at a price."

After these harsh words, Caspar's hand (so soft and manicured) gave Wakefield a comforting pat. "I'll raise the matter with the other Guardians. Leave your plan with me, Wakefield. And not a word to anyone."

As the next days passed, Wakefield pictured an offer being whispered to two identical brown faces, holding out to each Son the chance to become the sole living progeny of the great Pan-Gi, simply by uttering a single 'yes'. They won't agree, Wakefield told himself fervently; neither Tercero nor Primero! They're both good at heart; they'll both refuse, and he'd know at least that each was trustworthy.

Tears of regret streamed down Wakefield's face when Caspar, close to tears himself, told him sorrowfully that Tercero — Tercero! — had taken his bait. Who could believe, Wakefield thought bitterly, that such evil could lurk in the Pan-Gi's Son — for the Pan-Gi, whatever his weaknesses, would never have been capable of what his clone had done. Something in poor Tercero's queer, troubled life had decayed his soul ...

For all his sorrow, Wakefield had at least the cold comfort that his choice was made. "Primero" — he sent a one-word message to the OverSouls and to Government, and then withdrew, throwing himself into the frantically-pressured preparations for the colony. If the homesteaders had to leave before the Sons turned 33, the first catalyst rockets had to be sent at once: There was urgent work.

All that night, he stayed hunched at the table making plans and lists; he hardly turned his stiff, tired neck when, towards morning, Elsbeth padded near.

"Are you sure?" she whispered, touching his shoulder. "About Primero?"

He didn't answer, only withdrew his shoulder so that her hand slipped off. He didn't want to think about the Sons; and, as he told her too sharply, he had work to do. Work that never diminished no matter how much he did, that paid no attention to night or day. Too much work to meet the questions in Elsbeth's eyes; so much work, that he hardly felt the emptiness, months later, when she moved out.

Yet in all the long years that followed — even when other women briefly took her place in bed — still Wakefield never quite removed the few clothes she'd forgotten in a drawer.

VII Journey's End

Those long years of exhaustion, and crazy hope ... It was only when a much older Wakefield, slightly stooped and hair touched with gray, was roused at the pre-appointed time from his cryoberth (waking slowly to the thrill that at long, long last, he was physically near Saturn's unique small moon, Valinski's Moon, named for the woman who'd discovered it) — only then did a thought that had been dark and dormant rise like a bubble from long ago. Suppose, just suppose ... that Caspar hadn't done what he'd said ... This was the thought that Wakefield woke with, in the jubilant moment when his dreams were coming true.

With feet that felt like lumps of clay, he was running, galumphing through the ship, while everyone was waking excitedly — the Gi's followers whom he didn't know, and his own people, calling out to him ... This was his triumph, but he couldn't pause; instead, over and over, he called names in his head, Primero, Tercero, Primero, Tercero ... Until finally he was near enough to shout one name out loud.

"Primero!"

He came up breathlessly to the personage who was probably, by now (after their 14-month voyage), the OverSoul Pan-Gi's only surviving Son.

"Primero —"

He hadn't seen Primero since the day they'd met, and the younger man's face, amid a jubilant group, was ready for exultant congratulations. Instead, Wakefield blurted out, "Were you ever approached, years ago, by someone who offered you a chance to have Tercero killed?"

With misery, he watched the smile falter on Primero's face, followed by a too-long pause. Clearly, Primero was searching for the right answer — whether it was true or not; and this fact alone told Wakefield far too much (told him that, long ago, Primero might once have woven false tales about Tercero). Wakefield could almost see the brain behind the Gi's bright face try frantically to decipher, in this public moment, what this crazy question meant.

But Primero couldn't figure the puzzle out. He told the truth, with a nervous laugh: "Wakefield — I think your cryoberth gave you some crazy dream."

Crazy Dreamer, Tercero had called him: Tercero, who certainly by now had been divested of his strange short life. Wakefield's head felt thick with grief and guilt. Suddenly it seemed obvious that the Guardians, the Pan-Gi's devoted followers, would never have condoned the bizarre test that Caspar had pretended to implement.

But why had Caspar tricked him? he asked himself, walking numbly through the ship, as deep cold black spun by outside and the vessel heated up each moment with excitement. Had Caspar thought that Primero would be a stronger leader? Or had he thought that reclusive Tercero would stand some chance of being allowed to live? Or had he been pursuing some sort of self-interest — but what possible self-interest had been served by selecting Primero over Tercero?

He found Elsbeth: unthinkingly he'd come to her, despite their broken relationship, as if he'd gone back in time 11 years to the agony of his decision point. She was waking slowly, the only person still in her four-berth cubicle, still groggy as she sat on her cryoberth; but her arms went around him with no hesitation when he came close. She was kissing his forehead when Lyon's head poked in.

"Lyon?" she asked, with disbelief.

"Why not? I got dreams too, like anyone. Wake, I saw you come in here — hey, what's wrong?"

Wakefield drew in a long, unsteady breath. "Let me tell you a story, Lyon."

He told his tale; and when he described his clever ploy, Lyon's lips pursed into a disapproving "o", while Elsbeth put her head in both her hands.

"Oh, Wakefield," she said, "you should never have given that Caspar person the temptation to interfere like that!"

"But he didn't stand to gain anything!" Wakefield protested.

Outside the cubicle, a cheer went up: small dun-coloured Valinski's Moon could at last be seen with the naked eye. Wakefield should be joining the rest of the key people in the ship's control room, moving triumphantly through the ecstatic crowd, who were all drunk with a sense of history.

"I don't understand why he interfered," Elsbeth said gently, stroking his face. "But maybe people like you and I can't out-think the Caspars of the world."

Lyon had been sitting on the opposite bed, squinting hard at Wakefield's shoes; now hunched forward, he spoke with conviction. "You gave him a chance to leave his mark." The others stared. "He didn't care who went — just so he chose."

And suddenly, Wakefield understood: Caspar had been tempted by the act of choice itself. The same way that presidents made decisions they knew were flawed — thinking, dammit, someone had to act, and come what may, they'd left their stamp! The same way, maybe, that assassins shot presidents. A type of glandular compulsion perhaps: to deposit one's scent on history. A fascinating wrinkle on human behaviour that

Wakefield the bookworm understood, too late.

Wakefield got up; he kissed Elsbeth, both of them shaky. There had been other relationships, for each, these lonely years — none of them worth a mention, now. Together they moved gingerly toward the control room, with Lyon beside them like a loping pup; a cheer went up when Wakefield stepped into the crowded, happy room. He looked around and located Primero, who in turn was watching him with a huge public smile of partnership, but who was also wary-eyed and wondering what was in Wakefield's mind. How strange was life that Primero was Wakefield's partner; right hand and left hand, they would shape some kind of brave new world.

NICK BANTOCK

The only thing that Nick Bantock seems unable to do is explain what he does for a living. He creates "pop-up books and, well — they're like children's books for adults, except they aren't really children's books." He is too accomplished an artist to be passed off as a writer and too good a storyteller to be dismissed as an artist. The only way to really understand what he does is to pick up one of his books and play with it.

Bantock and his artist wife Kim Kasasian moved from London, England in 1985. Bantock had been an illustrator and book cover designer and had reached the top of his field. "Bored witless and frustrated by a constipated society," they decided to come to Canada "and everyone said Vancouver was the place." They discovered Bowen Island within months of their arrival.

In a tiny house bursting with creative energy — they maintained two careers while producing four children — Bantock penned his best-known work, the *Griffin and Sabine* Trilogy.

Reprinted in the following pages is Bantock's minature book commissioned and published by Stanley Marcus, of Neiman-Marcus fame. The original, a limited edition of 300 signed copies, is handset and leather bound and the illustrations are hand-tinted.

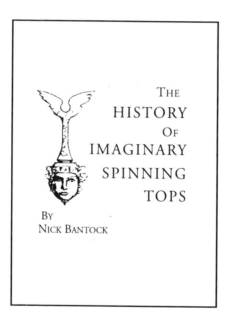

THE
HISTORY
OF
IMAGINARY
SPINNING
TOPS

BY
NICK BANTOCK

Howe Sounds

Published By
The Somesuch Press
Dallas, Texas

© Nick Bantock 1994
All Rights Reserved

' to my friends '

S HORTLY AFTER DISCOVERING the *Carmagh Spinning Stones,* the eminent archaeologist Thomas Westgatner stated that he was absolutely certain that spinning toys were the first playthings of Neolithic children.

Whether he was correct in his conclusions is a matter of conjecture. Certainly the diversity of topographies where spinning tops have been found,

• 1 •

from Aztec temples to Roman baths, suggests very early origins. Yet there really is no proof that these tops belonged to children.

It is impossible to know for certain whether the first tops were toys, gaming devices, methods of divination, or tools of ceremony.

Wishing firm ground under me, I've decided to begin this SHORT HISTORY OF SPINNING TOPS with the famous Sicmon Island Ceremonial Spinning Wheels. Their beginnings may be misty,

• 2 •

but their purpose and recent lineage are well documented.

Even better documented are the *modern* spinning tops, which may be separated into two (sometimes overlapping) genres: the plaything and the art object.

In Britain circa 1850 there began a trend, pioneered by one Bartholamew Wiltshire, to factory-fashioned spinning tops. However, as with so many innovations, it was not Wiltshire who benefitted from the ensuing craze but the entrepreneurs who followed him.

• 3 •

By 1900, the spinning top as a toy had lost its pull of the junior public imagination but it was saved from extinction by a new generation of artists and craftspeople who took the form as a means of self-expression. Thus was born "the golden age of tops" that fills the heart of this tiny volume.

• 4 •

SICMON ISLAND CEREMONIAL SPINNING WHEELS

The Sicmon Island ceremonial tops were first recorded by Charles Darwin in his *Beagle Logs*. According to the island's inhabitants, elders have "always" made spirit wheels; they are an integral part of Sicmon Islander's coming of age ceremony. Forty-nine tops, one for each year of the initiate's age, are simultaneously danced off a tiny pier-like structure into the ocean.

• 5 •

The Spirit Wheel opposite is a copy of a traditional design that dates back to the late eighteenth century.

The Spirit Wheel

BARTHOLAMEW WILTSHIRE
[1828-1887]

Born in Bradford, England, Bartholamew Wiltshire made his living as an engineer. He was the first to manufacture spinning tops for the mass market. However, his tops, which were cast iron, never found popular favour as they were rather weighty and tended to damage polished wood surfaces.

• 9 •

The Ionic Anvil is a classic example of the heavy-industrial design that reflected Wiltshire's Victorian sensibility.

The Ionic Anvil

WILLIAM MACKINTOSH
[1874-1950]

Cousin of the renowned Charles Rennie Mackintosh, William was an accomplished artist and designer in his own right. His interest in tops was short-lived, but in the five-year period between 1909 and 1914 he made over 50 beautiful and unique spinners.

• 13 •

Named after the famous Scottish railway engine, *The Fife Flyer* is a finely crafted top that incorporates brass and etched ivory.

The Fife Flyer

ANNA DE FORTE
[1895-1942]

Unquestionably the best of the Art Deco spinning top designers, Anna De Forte created tops suffused with an inimitable sophistication. De Forte inherited her family fortune when only sixteen, and used her privilege to expand her artistic talents. She was coached by the best French craftsmen and by her mid-twenties totally overshadowed her peers.

• 17 •

All De Forte's pieces were made from the highest quality metals. In the case of *The Firefly,* it is shaped from solid sterling silver.

The Firefly

JESSICA ST. PAUL
[1887-1963]

Of both French and native American ancestry, St. Paul grew up disliking and mistrusting humans. By nineteen, she was a hermit living deep in the forests of north Vancouver Island, Canada. Whilst clearing her cabin after her death, officials came upon a large pine chest that revealed hundreds of carefully crafted ceremonial tops. What induced her to make them no one knows.

• 21 •

Fox Tooth Totem is a typical example of a St. Paul "found object" spinner.

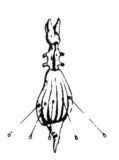

Fox Tooth Totem

GUNTER MARK
[1900-1945]

Mark was an idealist and his tops were rarely spinnable. They looked reasonable enough but his appalling sense of balance led him consistently to produce objects that would keel over within seconds. For years, he doggedly flogged at his chosen art but eventually his litany of failures began to unhinge his mind. He died in a drunken stupor in 1945, trying to descend a spiral staircase.

• 25 •

Made of brass, *Caxons Screw* makes a better paperweight than it does a spinning top.

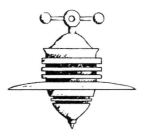

Caxons Screw

THOMAS ELLIS
[1901-1929]

Although an American, Ellis flew as a fighter pilot for the British during the last two years of the First World War. In the spring of 1918, he suffered a near fatal crash and lost both his legs. Having been given only a short time to live, he was sent back to New Hampshire to die quietly, but he clung to life for a further eleven years, spending his time building his trademark "aviation spinners."

• 29 •

Both elegant and functional, *The Rotator* utilizes a small propellor to prolong its motion.

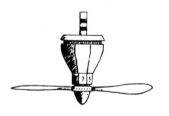

The Rotator

MARTIN PORCUBUS
[1898-   ]

Porcubus was a student of Mackintosh and his designs echo his master's style. Indeed, he still gives his tops Scottish names as a mark of respect. In recent years he's begun to experiment with modern materials such as fibreglass, but by his own confession he is a traditionalist. At ninety-six, he continues to build tops from his attic studio in Lisbon, Portugal.

• 33 •

The *Raith Whistle's* various tones of green are achieved by combining five materials from the apex: teak, copper, china, bone, and polished coal.

The Raith Whistle

BECAUSE OF THIS book's brevity, there are many fine makers of spinning tops who have not been included. I suggest that anyone wishing further information about those artisans should delve into the books listed on the following page.

BIBLIOGRAPHY

Barber, T. *Spinning Tops 1839 to 1939*
Deathe, M. *Top Turning*
De Forte, P. *Anna De Forte*
Fisherman, L. *Early Spinners*
Lenker, O. *Metal Spinning Tops*
Strohem, G. *Spirit Wheels of Sicmon*
Warboy, Y.B. *Post Industrial Spinning Tops*
Westgatner, T. *Digging in the Carmagh*

NOTA BENE: I once came upon a phrase, "the sense in nonsense." That term has become, for me, something of a beacon — the light I luxuriate in. I love it for the straightfaced humour it evokes, the playful way it chews at the edges of our inflated egos or bolsters our sagging self-confidence when the all-too-serious universe suggests that we among all mortals are *to blame*, and because it stops us from believing anyone who peddles musty dogma or fast food solutions designed to quell our rumbling stomachs.

Faced with the colour between yellow and red on the spectrum, out of a hundred people asked, thirty-three might tell you it is dark yellow, thirty-three might name it a bright red, thirty-three call it orange and one describes it as blue. Who is right and unconditionally reliable in sensory awareness?

This book pays homage to all those who never existed but should have done, if for no other reason than colour.

• 40 •

As well as to my previously mentioned friends, this book is dedicated to anyone prepared to say, with a twinkle in her or his eye, that orange is blue: be they mischievous or colour-blind.

Nick Bantock

JULIE OVENELL-CARTER

In the days before they were hyphenating and procreating, Julie Ovenell and Brad Carter were barely communicating, mostly because Julie wouldn't take Brad's calls. The Carter clan motto, however, is "Victory through patience" — Brad bribed Julie's lockermate at her Richmond high school for their combination and then left a rose in the locker every day for a year. The results can be seen in their two children, Adam, 3, and Kathryn, 6, and in a thriving Bowen-based writing business called Ovenell-Carter Communications.

Julie was born in England in 1960 and migrated to and around Western Canada at an early age. She obtained an Honours English degree at the University of British Columbia and a post-graduate Journalism degree at Carleton University in Ottawa before going into radio at CBC. Back in Vancouver, she worked in communications at the Canada Pavilion at Expo '86 and at MacMillan Bloedel before becoming senior editor at *The Globe and Mail's West* magazine. When the commute to her Bowen Island haven grew too onerous, she decided to pursue full-time the magazine writing that she had been doing on the side for most of her career.

She is now a regular contributor to *Canadian Living* magazine and splits her freelance work equally between magazine writing and corporate communications.

Food
Fight

At table, on Monday,
When Kathryn sat down,
She looked at her dinner
And said, with a frown:

"What *is* this disgusting brown horrible mess?
I suppose that it's food, but I won't even guess."
And she tipped up her nose, and she turned on her heel,
And she walked right away from her evening meal.

Came Tuesday, and supper,
And Kathryn came late
And she looked at the vegetables
Laid on her plate

And she said: "I can't stomach this mushy green stew.
This food is repulsive; it's the texture of glue."
And she stomped from the kitchen, went up to her room,
And curled on the bed, fell asleep in the gloom.

On Wednesday and Thursday
She had no better luck.
She looked at her dinner
And simply said, "Yuck."

    The cheese wasn't orange, the bread wasn't white,
    The beans weren't brown — there was nothing done
                                            right.
    She went to bed hungry for three nights, then four,
    And she dreamed about hot dogs, spaghetti, and more.

On Friday and Saturday
Kathryn was quiet,
But her tummy's rude noises
Were loud as a riot.

    She looked at the noodles, the rice, and the meat.
    She considered the plenty spread out there to eat.
    And she thought that just *maybe* she'd choke down a
                                          taste
    Since she'd hate to see so much bad food go to waste.

Then Sunday, at table,
When Kathryn came quick,
Her mom looked concerned,
Her dad thought she was sick.

    But sopping her gravy with a thick piece of bread,
    She looked at her parents and thoughtfully said:
    "I still don't think all food's a marvellous treat,
    But I don't like being hungry — so come on: let's eat!"

LISA HOBBS BIRNIE

Ten years ago, Lisa Hobbs Birnie was casting about the hallowed corridors of Ottawa, deciding people's fates as a full-time member of the National Parole Board. It was one of those federal appointments that prominent writers sometimes get, and it was fascinating for a time, but the call of the West Coast won out, and she and husband Wilf Birnie retreated to Bowen, where her son built them the island's only perfectly round house.

Australian born, Hobbs Birnie came to North America in the '60s and worked her way up through the newspaper trade, writing a column for the San Francisco *Examiner* and reporting from Vietnam and Cambodia for the *Chronicle*. She also spent a year studying at Stanford University on a Ford Foundation Fellowship. Coming to Canada in 1968, she wound up as an Associate Editor at *The Vancouver Sun*, writing editorials.

A contributing editor to *Saturday Night* magazine, Hobbs Birnie has also written seven books, two of which have been published in four languages. Her latest, *Uncommon Will*, a biography of Sue Rodriguez, is currently being translated into Japanese. Her next book, a collection of short stories, will be published in the fall of 1995.

Reflections
on the Light

My father died in remarkably comfortable circumstances. He had become a little unsteady on his feet, and his hearing wasn't the best, but otherwise he appeared to be in a state of permanent, and quite careless, good health. His memory was excellent and his interest in what was going on at home and abroad was more like that of an avid theatre-goer who never tired of opening nights, rather than that of an old man a few weeks short of ninety-seven.

He was an essentially kind man, urbane and non-judgmental. He had no need for rigid views and doctrines and tended to politely distance himself from those who did. A visit to India as a young man, however, had left him with three strong notions. One was the importance of keeping his spine ramrod straight, the second was the importance of breathing deeply, and the third was the futility of worrying about anything. This last notion, practical in application, was profoundly spiritual in source. The Indian air had seeped into his bones and left him with a permanent sense of being a tourist, a voyageur on planet Earth.

Three weeks before he died, he surprised his family by calmly announcing that he had had enough of life. In view of his age, this seemed reasonable, although it's fair to say none of us really expected him to take off quite as promptly as he did.

He remained cheerful, walking around the garden, sitting outside in the sun, chatting comfortably to anyone who dropped by. The only visible change was that he stopped watching the nightly television news and ceased reading his daily newspaper.

Eighteen days after making his own death announcement, his breathing became shallow and erratic, and he entered a small private hospital a short walk from his residence. He died there three days later.

The way in which he died has become part of the basic life data in my head. I can't call it information, for it lacks all the comforts of knowing. It's just data, something that happened, something that puzzles and fills me with impatience. My father seemed to die twice and both "deaths" occurred in an identical manner. My sister was with him the first time, chatting to him as he sat comfortably propped up in bed with pillows. Suddenly, in the middle of a sentence, he turned and, leaning slightly forward, looked to his right where there was a picture window opening onto a garden. His expression was one of an intense interest and surprise. He reached toward the window, as if pointing or welcoming, and then he died.

My sister called for help and a nurse rattled my father around until his poor heart started its habitual duties over again. It was probably as much against the nurse's will to revive him as it was against my father's wishes to be revived. On the following day, as soon as my sister had left, he seized his opportunity and promptly died. This time nothing was done to get the engine going again.

My sister was called immediately to the hospital, where she asked for the details of her father's death. The nurse said she and another nurse had been chatting to my father, joking with him about that evening's dinner menu, when he had suddenly leaned forward and turned his face to the window.

"It was very odd," the nurse said. "It was as if he saw someone there. He didn't look astonished, and he certainly wasn't frightened. He just looked very surprised, I'd say interested more than anything, profoundly interested and somehow pleased. He kept looking, and stretched out his hand as if in greeting. Then he stopped breathing."

Later I told a friend, who is a doctor, a highly trained technologist. He assured me that these were merely signs of the system shutting down. "The rush of light, all that sort of thing, it's merely the system turning off."

I laid this answer on top of the scene in my head and they had nothing to do with each other. An entire world separated them. I found my head simmering with pseudo-scientific questions and inexplicable longings. If it were merely the system turning off, why look in a certain direction? There could be physiological explanations for that. Even the expression of surprise could be explained by a sense of the body doing something it had never done before — relinquishing its life. But that look of interest, so keen, so intrigued, and so unmistakable in a face that had reflected interest all of its long life — what had caused that?

124

Some time later, I told the story to a Chinese friend. He said that there is a specific word in Chinese for this phenomenon. The calligraphy literally means, "the reflection of the light." What my father had seen, he said simply, was the reflection of the Source, or Spirit, or God, or whatever you want to call it.

I was stunned to learn that there was actually a specific word for this occurrence and when I met with a good friend, a Cambodian, who also happens to be a doctor, I was quick to share this little item. He replied that there is also a special word for this phenomenon in Cambodian. It literally translates as "the spirit coming to lead you to your next life."

I laid all this out before my brother in the hope of an answer, but he merely snorted and seized the opportunity to put me down. I was in danger of getting soft in the head, he said. If I went on at that rate, I'd soon be talking about Guardian Angels and all that rubbish.

Good grief! Guardian Angels! I'd forgotten all about them. I was schooled in a convent in times where there were more teachers than educators, when God was still alive, and everything was politically incorrect. Fanciful depictions of these androgynous beings with their delicate faces and eagle wings covered the schoolroom walls, hovering, protecting and guiding the soul-child in danger of earth's limitless evils — the rushing river, the cliff high above the sea, the hungry beast hiding in the forest.

Angels, in fact, were a big part of my early life. The nuns were apparently on intimate terms with them, mincing no words in describing their duties and ours. We were each given our own angel at birth: this angel had its own name but it was up to us to discover and own it. This angel stayed for life and if you listened to this spirit-guide, you would never lose your way. At death it would be your guide and companion into paradise.

Long ago I had ceased to believe in such things, so I cannot tell you how infuriated I was to find that with my father's death and my brother's words they began to roost in my head again, opening the door for my own reflections on the light and the coming of the spirit. My father had always brought me peace. How could he have left me with an impenetrable mystery, with an icon of his sweet dying face, filled with an interest that verged on incredulity, as his final, haunting legacy?

VALERIE LUPINI

At the age of 19, a career counsellor told Valerie Lupini that she should seek out a creative or literary career and that, at all costs, she should avoid technical or secretarial roles. She meandered off, studying at two colleges and four universities in British Columbia and Quebec before taking a series of jobs, all of them technical or secretarial.

Four years ago, she came to her senses and she has been writing ever since. Her work has appeared in newspapers *(The Vancouver Sun* and *The Globe and Mail)* and magazines *(Harrowsmith* and *Canadian Living),* and her first children's book, *There Goes the Neighbourhood,* is due for release in March 1995.

Her attachment to the Howe Sound region can be traced to the summers that she spent at her parents' cottage on Gambier Island. When she started a family of her own and began scouting for a safe and pretty place away from the city, it seemed natural to look at the neighbouring island of Bowen, where she now lives with her husband, Peter, and two boys, Jesse, 3, and Elliot, eight months.

The
B.A.F.U.
Club

A brother is born for adversity.
Proverbs 17:17

My pediatrician used to tell my mother that I looked like a child from the slums of Calcutta. In an attempt to increase my appetite when I was six years old, the doctor prescribed Vimicon. Every meal as that yellow Vimicon was spooned into my grimacing mouth, my older brother Basil began a rhythmic, "rrrrrunt juice, rrrunt juice, rrrunt juice..."

"You're not exactly Mr. Muscles," I would shoot back.

"At least I don't need rrrrrunt juice," he'd counter.

"Stop it, right now!" my mother would intervene. "Basil, do not call it runt juice anymore. That's the end of it."

"How about shrimp tonic ... shrimp tonic ... shrimp tonic..." he'd chant in crescendo until I'd burst into tears.

The truth is, I was small and skinny because I spent the first 10 years of my life trying to catch up to Basil and his friends. There were a few girls in the neighbourhood who would play school or skip with me, but I wanted Basil's company more than anything. I wanted to go with him to the vacant lot, to the store for candy, to his friend's houses. In an effort to keep up, I was constantly bruised, and had three broken collar bones and one concussion before my seventh birthday.

Recently, I read *Sibling Connections*, an article reprinted in the *Utne Reader* by Laura Markowitz. "We agonize over ups and downs with our parents, spouses and children, but mostly ignore one of our first and most primal bonds — our relationships with our brothers and sisters," writes Markowitz. "Brothers and sisters push buttons you'd forgotten you had, never forget humiliations and painful nicknames...."

Painful is right. As a child, it seemed to me that I had been born for target practice. Runt, Shrimp, and Skinny Bones were precursor's to more painful nicknames like Four Eyes, Brace Face and Flatsie. Like most children, I'd been taught that sticks and stones (not to mention being swung around by the arms and dropped on pavement) can break my bones, but names will never hurt me. But Basil's insidious name calling cut right through to my nerves and reduced me to tears every time.

He knew the buttons to push. Just by standing outside my closed bedroom door and creaking the hardwood floor boards, he would have me believe that the Little Brown Man, a creature of my nightmares who used to suck blood from my neck, had arrived.

... creak ... creak ...

"Ha, ha," I'd laugh. "I know that's you."

... creak ... creak ... creak...

"Bug off, you idiot. I know it's you, so go back to bed."

... creak ... creak ... creak ... creak ...

"Stop it! Get out of here or I'm telling Mum!"

... creak ... creak ... creak ... creak ... creak

"Muuuuum! Help me! Heeeeelp!"

At which point Basil would flash back to bed, close his door and feign sleep while I sobbed into my mother's arms that the Little Brown Man had come to suck blood from my neck.

For 10 years I endured his relentless teasing until we moved to a different neighbourhood where I made fast friends with two other skinny, flat-chested, horse-crazy girls. We three were a unified picket defence against Basil's bravado, which was becoming more offensive as he was now in the thick of puberty; two showers a day and inclined to wear a revolting aftershave after not much of a shave at all. His name-calling intensified as the chasm between us became more physically and emotionally pronounced. Claudia, Georgeann and I were Basil's ego terrorists, eager to find holes in his machismo armour. Then one day, we did.

My luck changed. I unearthed something from the bowels of Basil's bedroom which I carefully plucked out with a clothes peg. I wouldn't touch it, had trouble even carrying it close to my fingers. But to my amazement and delight, I had discovered a pair of Basil's underwear stained with what my mother used to call "skid marks."

"And what to my wondering eyes should appear!" I chortled as I swung the gem like a pendulum in front of Basil's startled eyes, "But a pair of white gonch and a pretty brown smear!"

Truly a nightmare for a male adolescent with a history of being not very nice to his younger sister — and favoured, I was certain, because he was older. Now was my chance to square things away. What good was the biggest bedroom now? After parading the underwear before the family in a cheer-leading style frenzy, I phoned Claudia and Georgeann for an emergency get-together. We met in Georgeann's bedroom, sitting cross-legged on her single bed with Skookum-Chuk the cat, a feline celebrity known around the neighbourhood for his ability to pee into the toilet bowl.

"Have you got them?" asked Claudia, inching into the huddle.

"Gross me out!" I said. "What am I supposed to do, put them in my pocket?"

"Oh, gross," said Georgeann. "Can we talk about something else."

"What else is there to talk about?" said Claudia. "Where are they?"

"Mum washed them."

"You turd," said Claudia. "Now we have zero evidence."

"I saw them! Dragged them out and actually, physically saw them."

"Gross," Georgeann yawned.

"What a pig," said Claudia.

"Tell me about it," I added with disdain.

So it was there, in Georgeann's bedroom, witnessed by one toilet-trained cat and a zillion horseback riding ribbons, where the B.A.F.U. Club, or the Beautiful Association for Underwear was formed. If anyone asked, it was the Beautiful Association for Underworld. Our mission statement was terse: to torment and embarrass Basil with the offending gonch.

The B.A.F.U. Club met once a week in a crawl space no bigger than a johnny-on-the-spot. Upstairs, through Mum and Dad's bedroom, out onto their porch and through a troll-sized door three of us trudged, then crouched under the sloping roof. Once inside, the door was closed and the B.A.F.U. Club was in session in the harsh light of Dad's electric lamp.

"Claudia?"

"Here."

"Georgeann?"

"Here."

"Me? Here. Okay. Everyone is officially present and accounted for. Whose turn to bring candy?"

Silence.

"I thought it was Clod's."

"I brought Ju Jubes last time."

"Who's secretary this week?"

Georgeann raised her hand.

"Read last week's minutes and I'll prove that it was Clod's turn to bring candy."

Claudia, leaning forward: "Don't bother, we don't have candy so let's get on with it. My back is killing me."

So there we sat cross-legged, knocking knees together on the old blue rug, staying well away from the walls where nails from the roof shingles poked in on us. We talked mostly about Basil's bad behaviour and how we could use the recent discovery to our advantage.

When he called me names, I would remind him of the underwear. When he wouldn't want to take me with him to Mac's Milk, I threatened to exhibit non-existent photographs of the underwear on strategic telephone poles in the area. Not only did he have to take me to the store, but he had to buy me the Pez dispenser of my choice. If he called me flat-chested, as he did (legitimately) until I was 15, I reminded him that although I may not be well-endowed, or endowed at all, I at least had some bowel control.

Perhaps the cruelest threat of all was that I might describe the whole incident to Wendy Swenson, a friend of Georgeann's who lived in Lake Oswego and visited every summer. Wendy was well-endowed because, Georgeann explained, "Her mother's got bazoos, too." My mother also had bazoos but I had obviously inherited them inside out.

Wendy was a blond, buxom babe with blue eyes and full lips who descended into our collectively scrawny midst every August. Her riding pants clung to her curves while mine sagged in the bum. Her teeth were white and straight while mine were bound in braces and retainer. In short, I would've been happy had Wendy just stayed in Lake Oswego.

Basil, on the other hand, was delighted and dumbstruck to see her, whipping up an interest in horses whenever Wendy waltzed around. This particular summer, however, I was also keen to have Wendy nearby. Whenever Basil ventured from his wheelbarrow of straw and manure, daring to dote on Wendy as she groomed her horse, I'd sidle up and make him squirm with sentences which began, "By the way Wendy, there's something I should tell you..."

Basil's face burst into blushing, as I continued, "... you won't believe what I found under Basil's bed..."

Sweat formed on his brow. Panic flashed across his face.

"... this cool book called *The Horse Owner's Manual* that belonged to my Granny and was written in 1908!"

As Claudia, Georgeann and I ran out of original remarks, we began to embellish the story. The underwear was unrecognizable until it had been dry cleaned, we decided. It had been left for weeks. Imagine the smell! Mold sprouted forth like mushrooms on a tree stump. For a glorious few months, the underwear became more and more horrifying until school started in the fall and the crawl space grew cold and damp.

But the B.A.F.U. Club served its purpose. Name-calling diminished to some extent, though in retrospect it was probably because Basil's interest in girls increased and he ignored me completely.

The year I turned 13, for example, he bought me a 95-cent blue, plastic piggy bank for Christmas. His girlfriend received a state of the art stereo system. Basil disappeared after Christmas breakfast to set up the stereo at her house, and I sorrowfully sought out the hurtin' songs from my cassette collection which I played on my portable Take N' Tape tape recorder. The Guess Who's, *No Time Left for You, On My Way to Better Things* seemed the only solace for my heavy heart.

The following Christmas was worse. We'd opened our presents in the morning, as usual. I was fully expecting a freebie from MacDonald's or one of my dad's office calendars from Basil. Instead, I was astonished to discover that he had beautifully gift-wrapped and given to me, his only sister, a Paddington Bear resplendent in rain coat and hat. Although we should have been past the teddy bear collecting stage, we each maintained a collection of childhood animals, adding a special bear from time to time.

Ironically, the Christmas season had fa la la la la'd itself right into my heart, and I had forgiven him for (or decided to forget about) past injustices. I'd spent $20, hard-earned from my first stable-cleaning job, on a beautiful teddy bear for his collection. Buying each other very nice bears seemed an act of sibling sensitivity. Was he trying to make up for the fact that our father's two childhood teddies, Tet-the-Ringle and Yellow Bear, had been handed down to the male child? Surely this signified a new era in our maturity. We were both capable of forgiving and giving.

Then the doorbell rang. Ding Dong. It was Mary Reeves, Basil's girlfriend of almost two weeks. She had come to give Basil a Christmas present and obviously expected one in return. Mary was led to the living room where she was left to grow giddy over the suggestion of a gift which had been carefully stowed away in Basil's bedroom.

"Be right back," I heard from the hall as Basil raced up the stairs and flew into my bedroom in a panic. "I need the Paddington!"

Mary Reeves left the house with my beautiful new bear tucked under her arm. I stormed into Basil's room, snatched up the bear I'd given to him, stomped back to my room, slammed the door onto his foot, screamed at him to get out and stay out of my room, slammed it again, then sulked and steamed while listening to the Guess Who's *She's Come Undone*.

Years later, when a bunch of us were helping my parents move from that house, Basil's girlfriend found the fluorescent orange B.A.F.U. Club sign in the crawl space.

"What's B.A.F.U. mean?" she asked.

Basil's eyes shot to me. Could it be that the B.A.F.U. still had some kick?

But true to the nature of our selective memory, it wasn't the chants of "rrrunt juice" that filled my head at that moment, so much as the log-rolling contests at the cottage, trading candy after Halloween and sitting together with our teddy bears at a little wooden table, all dressed up for a tea party.

"The Beautiful Association for Underworld," I said.

Less than a week later when I was visiting Basil at his apartment, I regretted the lost opportunity at revenge and short-sheeted his bed.

PASCAL GUILLON

Despite his Parisian birthplace — or maybe because of it, who knows? — Pascal Guillon is an admitted anglophile. He left Paris at the age of 16, travelling to England to go to school. In letters back to his parents, the nature of the "school" was never actually mentioned: "I told them I was learning English; I just never told them how."

In the next four years, he lived in the United States and Canada, and by the time he was 20 — "after you know everything, but before you discover that you are not immortal" — he was back travelling around Europe, in part doing resarch for this story.

In the years that followed, he worked in the Canadian merchant navy on all three coasts and in the Great Lakes, but in the off season he kept drifting back to the restaurant trade. That Parisian accent left no doubt in anyone's mind that he must know much about food. In fact, his only cooking job was on a construction site in England, where he learned "the finest British working-class culinary art." His wife, Lois, says that when they met, he cooked her his specialty: beans bourguignonne. She hasn't let him back into the kitchen since.

A reporter at Radio Canada in Vancouver since 1986, Guillon came to Bowen Island in 1988 to cover a story about the orchard cottages and "discovered what a beautiful place it is."

He never left.

Montenegro
by
Mistake

Christ! He is an ugly bugger, I thought as I looked at Alexis seated in front of me in the restaurant. His dirty black hair was the sad-looking victim of a homemade cut. His dark eyes held no hint of kindness or humour. His nose, crooked and flattened, proved that he preferred boxing to croquet. A scar on his upper lip and a few missing teeth reinforced that impression. He had a longer and nastier scar on his left cheek, as if he had been cut with a knife and then stitched up by a net-mending fisherman rather than a proper surgeon. His clothes were shapeless and ugly, even by the Yugoslav standards of the early '70s. His oversized, open jacket was sort of dark blue, as was his sweater underneath. I had noticed earlier how his jeans fitted badly and I thought they were probably a cheap Polish imitation of a Levi.

He asked again why I had chosen to come to Titograd. Alexis spoke broken English, rolling his R's like a KGB spy in an old American film. I explained, again, that I was travelling slowly and cheaply around Yugoslavia before going on to Greece and the Middle East. He shook his head, unable to comprehend why anyone would choose to waste his time away from the coastal resorts or the big cities.

"Now is November, is cold. It make raining all the time, is not nice," he said, looking puzzled.

He had a point, the place looked a bit grim.

"Anyway," he continued, pronouncing his 'w' as a 'v', "Yugoslavia is shit, and Montenegro is more shit than other parts, and Titograd is

135

number one capital of shit!"

"As I told you, I hadn't planned to come here," I reminded him. Indeed I had taken a bus in Belgrade, intending to travel to Sarajevo and then Dubrovnik, on the coast. In the coach station, someone with a warped sense of humour had assured me that I had to change buses in Titograd to get to Sarajevo. That is why I travelled all day and all night to Montenegro instead of going up to Bosnia-Herzegovina. The bus stopped in every single village along the way. Inasmuch as I had been able to see through the mud-splattered windows, I noticed that the rough and narrow road wound its way over the mountains, passing through poverty-stricken towns and villages, some of which were made up of old stone houses huddled around a mosque — a reminder of the Turkish influence that once extended far into southeastern Europe. At one point, when the bus shuddered to the summit of a mountain pass, one of the passengers tapped me on the shoulder, pointed to a distant valley below and said: "Albania!"

Once in the modern, grey-concrete warehouse that was the Titograd bus station, I realized that I had succeeded in getting off the beaten path. Outside, it was at least dry and sunny as I walked along a straight and dusty street, bordered by rows of three-storey concrete blocks of flats in which, I presumed, the liberated working class waited for the triumphant dawn of socialist utopia. I soon found myself in a park, or an expanse of yellowish grass beside a shallow river. Across the river, old buildings were gathered around a mosque. I bought a packet of Drava, cheap Yugoslav cigarettes, in a small kiosk of corrugated iron. I sat on a bench, turning my back on the unappealing modern Titograd, and looked at the old town across the river.

"If you had got a map, as I advised, you wouldn't be here," said the voice of reason, inside my head. It was a soft, but self-confident, feminine voice — infinitely patient, but occasionally exasperated by the talent I had for getting myself into absurd situations.

"Hello friend, you tourist?" asked a menacing-looking goon whose smile inspired as much confidence as a crocodile's.

That is how I met Alexis. I was glad to find someone who spoke some English. I asked him if he knew any cheap hotels nearby, but he said no, adding; "Only two big hotels here. Big money. Nothink cheap! Cheap tourist like you no come here!"

I knew right away that he didn't work for the tourist bureau. I also doubted that any kind of tourists, cheap or otherwise, came here in any significant number. The voice of reason started nagging again. "Surely you're not going to trust this bum. I mean, look at him! He'd scare the hell out of the Hell's Angels!" I had to admit that he didn't look like the sort you'd like to bring home for tea. I was about to find an excuse to take my leave without hurting Frankenstein's feelings, when the macho voice inside my head started giving me a hard time. "Don't be ridiculous! General Gordon held out 10 months during the siege of Khartoum, and you'd get frightened off by some Montenegran guttersnipe?" he asked, speaking in the short, sharp, clipped sentences of one who has better things to do than waste time with fools and cowards. He sounded very much as if he was James Bond's commanding officer.

I asked the boxing ape if he knew of a cheap restaurant, and it turned out that he didn't know any other kind. We walked through the modern Titograd, which was pure Eastern European modern drab relieved here and there by trees and flower pots. The shops were few and unappealing. Traffic jams were not yet invented as most people went about the town on foot. We turned off the main avenue into a narrower street where the restaurant was the only business on the block. It wasn't about to get a prize for fancy decor. There was flowery wallpaper and a dozen formica-topped tables with plastic and metal chairs in various unpleasant colours. Directly across from the front door, another door led to the kitchen, where loud Serbo-Croatian love songs oozed from a cracked radio speaker. I looked at the dusty portrait of Tito on one wall, and the yellowing colour photos of football stars on the other, and I followed Alexis to a table by the unwashed window. I looked at the flock of dead flies resting peacefully on the window sill and reflected that the vacuum cleaner was one bourgeois imperialist tool that was successfully kept out of the Federated Yugoslav Socialist Republics. "Never mind, dirt and dust never hurt anybody," snapped the small macho voice between my ears.

We were the only customers, and Alexis shouted in the direction of the kitchen, only to be answered by a distant grunt. There was apparently only one dish, and that being ordered, there I was, having a pleasant chat with the ape.

"Where did you learn to speak English, Alexis?"

"I work on boat. I goink everywhere: America, German, Arab places, Africa, all places I goink!"

"What are you doing back here?"

"Bastard police take my passport. I no can go out of Yugoslavia."

"Why did they do that?"

"They always make trouble for me. Somebody say something bad to me, so I box him a little. But he not strong. He going to sleep."

"You mean you knocked him out?"

"Well, what can I do? One little smack on face and I knock to sleep. Then police make trouble and take my passport. They don't like me because I am businessman."

"What sort of business?"

"Import business."

"Don't get sucked into any cheap smuggling deals," warned my voice of reason. Naturally, I ignored it. Instead, I looked at two other customers who came in and sat down at the opposite end of the room. It was a young couple. He was dressed like a Southern European worker wanting to look successful; black shiny Italian shoes, tight, black polyester trousers, loud shirt opened on a hairy chest, black jacket and hair slicked back with grease. She was tall, thin and, I thought, rather pretty in a rough and somewhat vulgar way.

"No look at her so much," whispered Alexis, "I no want to make boxing with that man, I no want trouble."

I could see his point, knowing that Mediterranean civil wars had started for less than that.

A fat Montenegran mama with a dirty apron emerged from the kitchen with two plates she deposited noisily in front of us. She was followed by a scruffy, unshaven, middle-aged man, with a cigarette in his mouth. He brought a basket of coarse bread and two opened bottles of beer. I contemplated the liquid mess in my plate. It appeared to be some sort of oily broth. A potato emerged in the middle of the slick, as an island of salvation in an ocean of fat. The bread was good and I mopped up the broth with it. Alexis devoured the food with loud slurps and a lot of lip-smacking. Later, the "businessman" ordered more bread and two plates containing raw tomatoes, raw onions, olives and a bit of goat cheese. Afterward, over coffee, cigarettes and plum brandy, I asked Alexis about his plans.

"I plannink all the time, no worry. After I buy passport I go live in Italy with my girlfriend. She crazy for Italy."

I paid for the meal, which was cheap in any case. And after Alexis said generously, "come stay in my house how much long you want!" what could I say?

Night had fallen by the time we went out in search of a taxi to take us chez Alexis. We found a cab, but Alexis soon got into a loud argument with the driver. There was a lot of arm-waving and only later did I realize that Titograd taxi drivers were not keen on going to Alexis' neighbourhood after dark. Or even in the middle of the day, actually. We finally got in the car, Alexis in the front giving directions. We drove quickly across the small city centre, then through a poorly lit district of small individual bare brick houses, and past a large dark building that could have been a factory or a warehouse before stopping in what seemed to be the edge of town. I paid the driver and then endeavoured to follow Alexis who walked ahead in the darkness without a word.

"Now you've really done it," said my voice of reason. "You're walking on a dirt road, in the middle of nowhere, with a violent criminal in search of money and a passport."

Even my macho voice seemed to lack confidence a bit, as it said, "Well, that's why you're travelling. You're in search of adventure, right?"

I could hear dogs barking in nearby houses. As we got closer, I could see in the moonlight that they were not exactly houses as much as shacks of various shapes and sizes. I managed to follow Alexis without tripping on the uneven ground. We passed through a garden gate made of wood and chicken wire. The fence was made from old car doors, rusty sheets of corrugated iron, bits of wooden crates, plywood and old tires.

"A reasonably clean and comfortable hotel would not have cost you more than $10 to $15," reminded my voice of reason. "Never mind the bollocks!" countered my macho voice. "You're here for adventure and not on some poxy organized tour to Disneyland."

I followed Alexis inside a small room, smelling of garlic, onions, sweat and stale tobacco. After a few seconds, I got used to the dim light cast by the petrol lamp. A coal stove gave off some heat. A counter, made of rehabilitated wooden planks, supported a stack of dirty dishes and a couple of plastic basins. Handmade rickety shelves ran along the walls. Close by the door, an old lady with dishevelled white hair sat at a metal kitchen table. She barely glanced up as we came in. She was busy rolling cigarettes from a big pile of raw tobacco heaped on a sheet of newspaper. Alexis talked to her roughly. She grunted without looking up.

"My mother will go sleep at house of brother. She get ready. Put your bag here. We go for drink."

I followed the Montenegran boxer through a labyrinth of dark and narrow alleys, where we raised a chorus of angry, underfed, chained dogs. As we approached a large disused industrial building, we were challenged by a couple of intimidating characters. They chatted with Alexis, examined me in the light of an electric torch, and talked some more to my host.

"Give them money," said Alexis. "Ten dinars is good enough."

Having paid this small "local tax," I followed Alexis inside a big industrial building transformed into a kind of bar. In the large, smoky rectangular room, men sat at rough wooden tables, played cards, talked, drank beer and plum brandy, or looked up at the silent black-and-white porno film projected on an old bed sheet hanging on a wall.

"I'm surprised things like this are allowed in Yugoslavia," I said to Alexis after we had sat down.

"Is not allowed, but here is special place. Police no come here at night. Police also no come here in day time. Here is special place for Titograd Albanians!"

"Are you Albanian, Alexis?"

"Yes my friend, all people here is Albanian. If you come here with

Alexis, is okay. If you come here alone, they beat you and take everything from you. If you fight back, they kill you, and nobody see nothink!"

"I see, it's a kind of autonomous region," I said, looking, I hoped, braver than I felt. It is hard to remember the rest of the evening. There was far too much brandy and beer, which I paid for. Soon after we arrived, we were joined by a rough and tough, but good-looking, short-haired young woman, whom Alexis introduced as Gina, his girl friend.

"She is number one pickpocket in Yugoslavia," Alexis said with pride. "She want to go Italy. She crazy for Italian."

My inner voice of wisdom kept nagging at me: "You're getting drunk, in a place where you'd better be wide awake! How can you be that stupid?" My macho voice sounded to me much less credible when it said: "You finally got where no tourist ever got before, an Albanian slum in darkest Montenegro. Boy! That's real adventure!" I only hoped that I could get out of it in good enough shape to be able to brag about it.

Then, I remembered Alexis' face, intense and uncomfortably close to mine, as he asked: "Make import business with me my friend, you and me we can make money and go Italy to live good life!"

"What sort of business?"

"You go with Gina, here, on ferry to Italy. Then she tell you what you can buy. After you come back with her. Yugoslav custom man no look your bag because you are Western tourist, so is normal you have Western things in bag."

"Then what?"

"Then we sell those things here, we make money, Alexis buy passport, we go Italy and make good life."

"How do we live in Italy?"

"We go Roma, many tourists, Gina take everything from pockets. Is easy."

"What makes you think you can trust me, Alexis?"

"You are sailor, same like me, you and me too much friend!"

I had told Alexis that I also worked on ships, but I don't think the Canadian coastal vessels I worked on had much in common with the floating sweatshops of doubtful registry that employed the likes of Alexis. My voice of reason told me, predictably, that I was a fool. As I shook hands with Alexis, sealing a bargain that I did not intend to keep, my macho voice whispered, "Well done lad, go to Italy with the girl, and when you're there, you can leave her and take a boat to Greece. You can fool that Albanian monkey easily."

As if he was reading my thought, Alexis put his head close to mine, gave me a vicious grin and said slowly, "I also trust you because you understand that I kill people who try to play stupid games with Alexis."

I woke up back in the shack, where I laid, fully clothed, on a camp bed. Alexis was sitting on a crate, next to the rickety table that was the one-room shack's main piece of furniture. The Albanian looked rough, and I felt as bad as he looked.

"Get up, we have to meet somebody," he grunted.

As we left the shack, I was blinded by the bright sunshine. I looked at my watch and saw that it was close to eleven. Alexis secured the front door with a chain and a padlock, and I wondered what there was to protect from thieves. He swore, and reopened the door, having forgotten his cigarettes inside. As he came back out, I locked the place up for him and slipped the key in my pocket. I hadn't planned to do that. I just did it absent-mindedly. We were silent as we walked through the now crowded and lively shantytown. Everyone was staring at the man in foreign clothes that followed Alexis. We walked through a hole in the fence and entered the perimeter of a disused airfield where the grass had been kept short by numerous grazing sheep. Even my inner voices kept quiet, probably because they were as hung over as I was.

Barely glancing up to the mountains, seemingly so close, I followed the Albanian bandit out of the old airfield, through parts of the new town, across the park, over the bridge and into the winding cobble-stone streets of the old town. We entered a dark cafe, where Alexis went to sit down at a table already occupied by someone looking very much like Saddam Hussein. I sat down and Alexis said: "This is my cousin. He speaks English good, he work in England many years. Tomorrow, he go with you to Italy."

I just nodded, too stunned to ask any questions of Alexis, who didn't seem to expect any. The two Albanians talked for a bit. Small cups of Turkish coffee were brought and my "host" left us to go to the loo.

"So, tell me again what it is we're going to bring back from Italy?" I asked Saddam, although I don't remember ever being told the nature of Alexis' import business.

"Eleven handguns, a tape recorder, some watches and some other small crap like that," my designated travelling companion answered with an accent that suggested he spent quite some time in the not-so-fancy parts of London.

I nodded calmly, while inside my head, my inner voice of reason woke up suddenly, saying; "Now you've really done it you silly bugger! Next thing you know, they're going to ask you to hand over your passport to the Anglo-Yugo-Albanian thug so he can go and buy the tickets and they'll keep a close eye on you from then on. They'll probably keep your passport right up to the moment of embarkation. That'll be your last chance. You'll have to run up to a couple of border guard and seek their protection, while Saddam will probably pretend he doesn't know you and is not travelling with you." "Well, now, there is no need to panic," said my macho voice. "There is certainly no need to even think about going to the cops who are probably a bunch of Stalinist goons who would keep you in jail until they can sort it all out anyway. I admit it's looking a bit dicey, but we'll find a way out. In the meanwhile, we must keep a stiff upper lip, show those foreigners what we're made of."

Alexis came back, and it was my turn to go to the loo. It was in a small courtyard in the shade of a tall stone wall. There was an old wooden door in the wall. Instead of going inside the toilet stall, I walked to that door, pushed it open and saw that it led to a narrow back alley and freedom.

"Go for it," said the wise voice. "I fully agree," added my macho voice. I stepped into the alley, walked fast, and then a bit faster. In seconds I was on the bridge that led to the park and the new town. As I crossed the park, I made an effort to keep myself from running. As I had hoped, I saw a taxi parked in front of Titograd's big hotel. The driver spoke no English but was quite willing to go where I pointed. As we got close to the slum, the driver of the old battered Fiat taxi, grinned salaciously, said some rude words in German, elbowed me in the rib, winked and let go of the wheel so as to allow his hands to follow the contours of an imaginary woman. Why else would an outsider go to this slum, if not to visit some whore? The taxi stopped close to Alexis' shack. I gestured to the driver to wait, and noticed he looked a bit nervous. As I walked hurriedly to the shack, some of Alexis' neighbours called out to me. I smiled, waved back, pointed towards the town and shouted Alexis' name. I unlocked the door, got inside, grabbed my bag, and walked out, only to find the way out blocked by Alexis' old mum. I pushed past her, and walked away as she called out to the neighbours. I got inside the cab just in time, as the driver, not liking the look of some of the locals, was about to leave, even without having been paid. As we got farther from the shantytown, the driver and I relaxed a bit.

"To the airport," I said, indicating with mimes, an airplane taking off. Passing a travel agency on the day I arrived in Titograd, I had noticed a poster in several languages, including English, indicating there was a number of flights every day to Belgrade. The driver pointed at the clock and indicated there was lots of time for the Belgrade plane. I started to worry about the cost. Short plane rides within Europe can easily be beyond the budget of young travellers with backpacks. I showed the driver traveller's cheques and asked him if I could change them in the airport.

"Nein! Bank! Hotel!" said the driver, immediately making a U-turn on the empty road. As we got closer to Titograd, my worries increased. Alexis was bound to search for me, furious that I had wrecked his plans. All he had to do was send someone back to his place, thinking that I would go there for my bag, and hang around himself in the small down-town area where a foreigner was bound to stand out. As we arrived close to the hotel, sure enough, I saw Alexis walking away from the front door. I sank down on my seat, as low as I could, hoping not to be noticed. The driver seemed to understand that I feared the big guy walking away in the ill-fitting clothes. Alexis did not turn around, and I went from the taxi to the hotel lobby without being seen.

In the best of Eastern European traditions, something as simple as cashing traveller's cheque took a very long time. The hotel staff had to go in search of the cashier, who came down slowly and took forever to locate the appropriate forms to fill out. As I walked out of the hotel, Alexis was returning and he saw me immediately. He waved and shouted. I jumped inside the cab and yelled at the driver to go at once. Before he could get to the street, he had to stop the car to let a group of pedestrians cross the hotel driveway. That gave enough time for Alexis to grab the handle of the front passenger door. In my panic I had been unable to lock it and it was with horror that I felt Alexis' big hand grab my arm to pull me out of the car. The taxi left in a cloud of burnt rubber, the pedestrians turning to see the reason for the squealing tires. Alexis was pulled off balance and, losing his grip on my arm, he fell on the driveway. I was starting to feel a surge of relief and excitement as we got further away from danger, when the driver suddenly stopped the car.

"Dinar! Dinar!" he shouted, demanding to be paid immediately. He knew that I was willing to pay just about anything not to be abandoned in downtown Titograd with an enraged Alexis bent on murder. I was made to fork out nearly twenty dollars, a big sum in Yugoslavia in the early '70s. As the plane took off and I watched Titograd disappear, I started to relax. The many hours spent in the small airport had been tense. The passengers fought their way to the counter, opened at the last moment. Internal flights didn't seem to bother with reservations. I got the last seat, after I successfully elbowed an old lady away from the ticket counter. As it turned out, the flight was so outrageously subsidized that it cost less than the taxi ride to the airport. As we turned sharply over the mountains and started our short flight to Belgrade, a sarcastic feminine inner voice said: "So much for your adventures off the beaten tracks."

"For a moment there," rejoined the macho one, "I thought you were about to get into some serious adventure. But now, you're back to being your usual cowardly self."

Reassured, I smiled, laid back, and enjoyed the flight.

143

JIM KEARNEY

It is the great good fortune of Vancouver newspaper and radio fans that at the beginning of the Second World War, the Canadian military had one look at the "skinny, underweight, nearsighted" Jim Kearney and pronounced him unfit for service. Kearney was left with no choice but to seek work at the *Victoria Times,* which launched him into a journalism career that has lasted more than 50 years.

Kearney went on to work at *The Vancouver Sun,* Canadian Press in Toronto, *The Vancouver News Herald,* Reuters and the Central Office of Information in London, and *The Province,* back in Vancouver. Tempted by the big money of public relations, he moved to Westcoast Transmission in 1961, but by 1963 he was back at *The Sun,* where he was a daily sports columnist for the next 17 years. During that time, he also began his CBC radio editorials, which he continues to do weekly on the *Early Edition.*

The move to Bowen Island in 1986 was his second attempt to flee the big city. The first time, in 1956, he stopped at the remote community of Horseshoe Bay. "There was no highway, no railway and just a couple of little Blackball ferries. We used to swim where Sewell's Marina is now and my kids would play on the beach."

Those were …

The
Good Old
Days

Some of the boys were whooping it up — not in Robert Service's Malemute Saloon — but in the Bowen Island house belonging to Hughie Watson's grandmother. She wasn't there, of course, but Hughie was — leading, as it happened, a rather bibulous discussion group. .

The subject, long before Pierre Berton's latest book, was the feasibility of going over Niagara Falls in a barrel and living to tell about it. Watson was leading the argument for the affirmative and getting nowhere when one of the group suggested an empirical solution:

There was a rain barrel at one corner of the house. How about wrestling it onto the roof, stuffing Hughie inside and rolling it off? "Splendid idea," or something to that effect, said Watson, and the experiment was on.

All it cost Hughie were two broken ribs, but he took immediate consolation in the fact that he won the argument. Just another day in the life of one of Vancouver's great characters.

Because memory is very selective and tends to screen out most of the unhappy things, we old farts tend to dwell upon the good old days. They weren't good really, but they had a few good things going for them. I think we laughed a lot more. We didn't take ourselves too seriously. Political correctness hadn't yet been invented. Income tax was less onerous. And we seemed to be a lot more tolerant of the offbeat and outrageous characters who inhabited our business.

That would be the newspaper business, where Watson and I were contemporaries and spent about a decade working in the same sports department at *The Province*.

Challenging authority was one of his specialties. Ingenuity was another. There was the day when a nettled Erwin Swangard, then the sports editor, ordered Watson's byline struck forever. Watson retaliated in his next story. Reading vertically, the first letters in the 11 paragraphs just happened to spell By HUGH WATSON. Swangard exacted immediate revenge, assigning Hughie to the Swangard house as a babysitter. That, too, was a loser for Erwin. His liquor cabinet took such a beating that Watson was soon back covering hockey.

Erwin soon moved across the street to become sports editor at *The Sun*, and must have thought that his problems with Watson were over. He thought wrong. Hughie got his ultimate revenge by inventing the fictitious Howe Sound Basketball League. This was the fall of 1951 and he placed teams at such outports as Horseshoe Bay, Britannia Beach, Squamish, Woodfibre, Port Mellon, Gibsons and, of course, Bowen Island. And he invented a scoring star named Len Schwartz.

A friend, whose voice wouldn't be recognized, dutifully phoned in the scores two or three nights a week. As Erwin took the hook, running the first few instalments, the friend even phoned to praise *The Sun* for supporting community sports, promising in future to file to that paper exclusively. Just to round things out, every second week or so, Hughie would send along the revised standings and the up-to-date scoring race, which showed the mighty Schwartz averaging about 25 points a game.

The scheme was playing out so well that Hughie booked a hall for the end-of-season awards presentations, where Erwin would be invited as guest of honour. The denizens of *The Province* sports department all planned to be in attendance for Erwin's embarrassed arrival.

But Schwartz's scoring streak proved to be the league's undoing. The Canadian Amateur Basketball Association was in the process of selecting the team to represent Canada at the 1952 Olympics in Helsinki. Schwartz was on the short list, but the basketball authorities couldn't find him. Eventually they discovered there was no such league and no such player. And Swangard, poor guy, found himself on the carpet in the office of a carnivorous managing editor.

Watson eventually left *The Province* a winner over then-managing editor Mervin Moore. Behind in his alimony payments and needing some instant cash, Watson demanded that Moore fire him so he could collect severance pay. Moore kept refusing until one night, in the old Newsmen's Club on Georgia Street, they got physical about it.

Hughie wound up sitting on Moore's chest and refused to get off until Merv fired him and put it in writing. So, he got his severance money, made the alimony payments, rounded up an old drinking buddy and off they went to Waikiki, where he blew it all in a month.

But not until the two fell in, at a bar one evening, with a stranger, an English actor who had just flown in from Los Angeles, where he had got bored waiting to hear about his Academy Award nomination.

Miraculously, he came to no harm, except having to sleep on the floor in Watson's hotel room, Hughie and his buddy having appropriated the beds. But Albert Finney didn't seem to mind any more than he minded not winning an Oscar for the title role in Tom Jones.

On his return to Vancouver, Watson strayed into new careers as a publicist for the then-minor league Vancouver Canucks, publisher of a Howe Street tip sheet and, eventually, a taxi-franchise owner.

It was the Howe Street connection that led him to the place that he now calls home. One of his clients, who owed him $10,000, suggested that Hughie meet him in Puerto Vallarta because, for reasons never specified, the client couldn't come back to Canada. So Hughie went south, collected the 10 grand and slapped it into a Mexican bank that just happened to be offering 50-per-cent interest on savings accounts.

"Watson," said I, "you have to be crazier than I thought you were. Fifty per cent? That place could be out of business in no time at all."

"I look at it this way," he replied. "The interest will pay for a six-month vacation there every winter. Even if it goes out of business two years from now, I'll come out ahead."

The Bank of Mexico is still in business.

In a life full of nonsense, the only thing Hughie was serious about was sailing. A competent mariner, he started sailing to Bowen in his own dinghy at a time when the Union Steamship Company was still featuring Saturday night dance cruises from downtown Vancouver to Snug Cove aboard the SS Lady Alexandra.

It was a good thing he had his own transportation because the steamship line wasn't one of his big fans. He was the guy, some of the old timers remember, who, as the Lady Alex was backing away from the dock one midnight on the return leg of the dance cruise, came rushing down the hill and across the dock, yelling, "Wait for me! Wait for me!"

He was carrying an old suitcase, just for effect, and he just kept running, legs pumping wildly in the air, as he tried to long jump the 20-foot gap to the ship. As he swam under water to a hiding place behind a piling, a lifeboat was lowered and the futile search went on for an hour. Understandably, this was a one-time stunt.

Now well into his 60s and a non-drinker, Hughie no longer gets into trouble. Early in the '90s, he sold his cab franchises, his West End condo and, eventually the 26-foot sailboat that he and his wife, Rose, lived on during their summer visits, and retired to his Mexican haven.

RICHARD LITTLEMORE

Richard Littlemore fell into a writing career when his uncle, Robert Littlemore, tempted him into the newspaper business with a summer job at the *Ottawa Citizen*. Having felt the rush of ink in his veins, Littlemore worked his way west, stopping at *The Brandon Sun, The Winnipeg Tribune, The Winnipeg Sun* and *The Edmonton Sun*. Since 1984, he has worked at *The Vancouver Sun*, first as foreign editor and later as an editorial writer specializing in foreign affairs.

Littlemore says the two best decisions he has made were "marrying Elizabeth and moving to Bowen Island," where they now live with their three boys, Teddy, 3, Avery, 2, and Llewellyn, 1.

With this anthology, he makes his first foray into both book publishing and, for want of a better term, fiction writing. He would like to dedicate that effort to the honour of his father, George Littlemore, and the memory of his mother, Vicky.

How Now
Brown Cow?

I haven't always taken my father's advice.

This serves to distinguish him among men much more than me. The world is overburdened with sons who are determined to make their own mistakes, but few are the fathers who can resist the temptation to talk them out of it. My father is one of these. With only two exceptions that I can remember, he never told me what to do.

That's not to say that he left me entirely without guidance, but he barely ever invoked actual words to make his point. At a time before the term "body language" had found its way into the vernacular, my father could communicate his every preference with an encyclopedic vocabulary of gestures — the cocked eyebrow, the curled lip, the head tilted at that certain, disapproving angle. There was the smile, the pat on the back; but there was also the terrifying violence of the furrowed brow, folds of skin crowding together like so many stormy clouds. That look could bring me to a cold halt from the far side of a parade square, even as the legions marched between us.

If you leave aside the affectionate mussing of hair, this is exactly the vocabulary that most men use when communicating with one another. Of course, it's necessary to exchange the trivia of day-to-day life through the spoken word, and it's entertaining to chat about things that no one takes seriously — sports and politics. But when it comes to the crunch, most men will sign off with a gesture, knowing as they do that the new-age preoccupation with emotional honesty is both overrated and unnecessarily risky.

My sister has always been bugged by this, this failure between my father and me to forage into the corners of the other's consciousness. She thinks we are unable to communicate our deepest feelings, not merely unwilling. She would have us using the "l"-word, thinking that this sentiment is not otherwise expressed.

Seriously, when my father and I get together and look into each other's eyes and give one another one of those decisive handshakes — one up, one down, break — well, it would be redundant to tell the guy that I'm darned fond of him, and, I'm sure, he of me. Besides, this isn't merely a question of being drawn into some gushing, excruciating bit of men's movement melodrama. What would happen if we embarked on this odyssey of honesty and the conversation shifted from why-I've-always-loved-you-Dad to the seven or 12 things we have never discussed because we feared we may come to blows? We would already be too far down the path to prevent the evening ending in a fit of communal crying — which is out of the question — or an even less appropriate display of temper.

This brings me back to the topic, which is fatherly advice, and the examples, which on both occasions had to do with fighting.

Of course, every boy gets the same advice on fighting: Don't. This, I think, generally comes from your mother and is accompanied by a host of impractical platitudes about the greater courage shown by boys who turn their backs on conflict.

I knew the drill, but somehow it never seemed relevant when the tempers started to flare in the school yard. I would always stand my ground and work up my fiercest scowl — a bit of body language that always seemed to work, thanks to the happy circumstance that I was generally the biggest kid in my class. Thus, I was unpractised and overconfident when, walking home from school one day, I stumbled upon a fight in progress. I can't remember if I was in Grade 1 or Grade 2. I can't remember the name of my nemesis or the name of the kid he was beating up when I arrived. All I recall is that it seemed unfair and therefore incumbent upon me to step in and break it up.

This I accomplished easily. The aggressor turned immediately from his victim and started toward me, swinging his arms like a two-winged windmill. He was crying, out of control. I was composed and most assuredly in the right. I stuck out my fists, as I fancied I should, tilted my head way back — to be farther from the flurry of blows — and met his advance. He cracked me sharply on the bridge of the nose, bringing the tears to my eyes even before I could start to cry. And then he ran.

This was yet more unfair. Here I was, standing on the burnt summer plain in Wainwright, Alberta. I had right on my side, I was a lot bigger than the other kid, and I was surely a nicer guy. And yet I had just lost my first fight. It just didn't seem possible.

I was still crying when I got home, the fluids pouring equally from my eyes and nose. My mother patched me up with a Kleenex and a hug and turned me over to my father. He listened gravely to the details of my story and then said: "Well, there you go. You had it all wrong.

"Listen. Next time some guy comes at you like that, instead of leaning back and exposing your nose, what you should do is bend right down, get your chin on your chest and your head real low, and then run at him. While he's punching you on the back, which doesn't hurt much, you hit him in the stomach. That'll get him."

I was stunned. This was my father, a man of the richest moral fibre, a professional peacekeeper who had held off antagonists from Korea to the Gaza Strip. I had expected him to call the military police, or at the very least summon the villain's father and demand justice. Instead I get Chapter One from *Growing Up With Rocky Balboa.*

It was a classic example of the mixed messages that boys get about fighting. The first bit of advice is: Don't. The second is: And when you *do,* don't lose. I wanted to cry out, to demand that the world stop turning. John Wayne won all his fights. So did the Lone Ranger and Zorro! Was it all a fraud?

Mostly, though, I wanted that kid — or any kid — to run at me like that again, arms flailing, belly waiting. I'd get him next time. Next time I would know. But the boy avoided me warily for weeks and I probably avoided him, my nose still being a bit tender. And in all the fights I went on to lose in later childhood, no one ever beat me up the same way twice. Like much good advice, it applied only to a situation that was never to be repeated.

My father's second offer of pugilistic counsel came some years later in the form of a parable. I was likely not paying much attention, and Father is economical with his story telling, so I suppose, given the vividness of my recollection, that I have recreated most of the detail in my own mind, just as one recreates a joke around a known punchline.

But I can see the scene and smell the dust in the air. It's another one of those bleak prairie scapes, only this time during the Depression. Near as I can tell, the first guy to dub the Thirties "dirty" lived in my father's neighbourhood. North Regina, six or eight blocks beyond the last streetcar stop, hardly put up enough resistance to make the wind whistle. Although subdivided into municipal parcels, the area was still too sparsely developed to justify the term urban. Dusty, scrub-covered lots separated most houses, which were themselves stunted and dulled by the incessant, gritty wind.

In one such house lived my father's family. George, my dad, was the eldest of three boys — an older half-brother having already moved away from home — and thus he bore the heavy burden of premature responsibility. He was the one who had to do most of the work when the brothers made apple pie on Saturday afternoons. And he was the one who took the worst licking when his parents got home and discovered not only that the boys had made pie, but that they had eaten everything but the crumbs on the living-room carpet.

George's younger siblings were much as you'd expect from any birth-order study: Bob, an easy-going middle child, glib and quick to find compromise; and Billy, a bold and mischievous youngest, accustomed to indulgence within the house and protection without. What are older brothers for?

Past this house, morning and evening, walked another young boy — at 10 or 11 he would have been about the same age as Bob. In such a neighbourhood, a regular pedestrian would have been noticeable enough, but this one was leading a cow, out beyond the last of the scattered houses and into the fields to graze and then back to the tiny stable behind his own home.

If this picture was filmed by Bergman or Fellini, it would be all sadness and stoicism, a skinny young boy pulling at a lean and filthy brown cow. Both boy and cow would be braced against the biting wind, and the rushing tumbleweeds would seem to taunt them for their plodding pace.

But the audience in my father's house, three boys who had never had to walk a cow, saw this scene through the lens of the Marx Brothers or Mel Brooks.

"Hey, *cow* boy, where are the Indians?" they would call.

"Hey, Little Boy Blue, where's your horn?"

"Hey, Elsie, who's your friend?"

Most of this would come from the youngest, Billy, who could summon an inexhaustible supply of these juvenile insults. But the cow boy maintained his Bergmanesque stoicism, neither tarrying to counter the banter nor hurrying to avoid it. Which, of course, couldn't last.

Billy arrived home from school one day, two buttons popped from his shirt, and a great swollen scrape where his smirk used to be. He had been harrying the cow boy in the school yard, amid that most cruel and fickle of audiences, and he had, finally, gone too far.

George knew instantly what must be done; family honour demanded that such a thrashing must be avenged. Billy may have provoked the battle, but he was younger and smaller than the cow boy. And while Bob would have provided the fairer match, George's intervention ensured that the point would be made, and made convincingly.

The next day in the school yard, the combatants arranged the hour of retribution: "When your done dallying with your smelly old cow,"

George said, "I'll be waiting."

The cow boy never flinched, and sure enough, after his evening duties, he reported to meet the challenge.

Here, then, is the image of lost honour. Two unwilling adversaries toe to toe, fists out, chins down, circling in a style that would have made the Marquis of Queensberry proud. For this was surely an age when two such boys would never have considered "fighting dirty." Long before kick-boxing and far from the knowledge of Kung Fu, they would rather have insulted their own mothers than hit below the belt or use their feet for anything but dancing.

There was a small crowd gathered — though no one stood in the cow boy's corner — and while everyone was boisterous at the outset, the longer the two opponents shuffled and jabbed, the more silent the spectators became. There was only the quiet chorus of "ooh" and "ahhh" whenever one of the two fighters landed a blow.

George, determined and confident, was working away, looking for his opportunity, when he let a punch dangle a bit too long and the cow boy grabbed him by the wrist.

It was vice-like, that grip. Here was the only boy in the neighbourhood who had his fill of milk and cheese and he was attached to George's arm like an overtightened manacle. The scene became surreal. Looking at his own wrist, George could only imagine the stout rope that he had seen in the cow boy's hand so often. Looking at his antagonist, George could only remember all those dusky winter evenings when he had watched the cow boy pulling and coaxing 800 pounds of beef down a snowy street.

The cow boy suddenly yanked George's arm, trying to bring him around for a headlock and both boys went down with a thud. The force of the fall broke the cow boy's hold and the two began wrestling and scrabbling in the dust. The crowd erupted, the brothers yelling desperate encouragement — "C'mon George, get him!" — but it seemed that every time George got into a position where his larger size and better leverage would give him the advantage, he would feel again the strength and tenacity of his rival. Over and over again he was pushed back, pulled down and finally squeezed between sinewy thighs.

The cow boy took total control. His legs locked around George's torso, he rolled him face down and twisted one arm up to the screaming point. Then he grabbed a big handful of curly dark hair and gave a firm push, grinding George's nose into the dirt.

Fights always seem to last longer when you are in them, and this is a fight's longest moment. Though fleeting in real time, you have a limitless opportunity to consider questions of fairness and justice, of failed tactics and chances lost. Thus, in the course of introducing the cow boy to every "uncle!" on either side of the family, George had ample time to think about the injustice of his youngest brother's cause.

Yes, they had been a bit tough on the cow boy. His was not an easy life and he deserved a little respect from his neighbours. Besides, what a pleasure it must be to have fresh milk in the city. How wrong they had been to see anything funny in the cow boy's labours.

At the exact moment when the crowd might have been expected to set upon the aggressor to end the fight, the cow boy stood up. George, too, picked himself up, blowing a considerable amount of prairie out of one stuffed nostril and dabbing gingerly at the new abrasion across his forehead. Without further unpleasantries, the crowd dispersed.

• • •

As I said earlier, much of this story is as I imagined it. Though I now have three boys of my own and can guess at the elements of brotherly interaction, I cannot seriously muster a vision of my father as anything but a responsible adult. I certainly can't conceive of him dwelling on these details. In fact, as I recall, he merely sketched a brief outline and then offered that second, concise bit of advice:

"Never pick a fight with a guy who has to walk his cow twice a day."

And, just for the record, I never have.